THE BRITISH LIBRARY
HISTORIC LIVES

Horatio Lord Nelson

THE BRITISH LIBRARY
HISTORIC LIVES

Horatio Lord Nelson

Brian Lavery

NEW YORK UNIVERSITY PRESS
Washington Square, New York

First published in Great Britain
in 2003 by
The British Library
96 Euston Road, London NW1 2DB

Designed and typeset by
Andrew Barron @ thextension

Printed in Hong Kong
by South Sea International Press

First published in the U.S.A.
in 2003 by
NEW YORK UNIVERSITY PRESS
Washington Square, New York
www.nyupress.org

Library of Congress Cataloging-in-
Publication Data
Lavery, Brian
Horatio Lord Nelson/by Brian
Lavery
p. cm. -(The British Library historic
lives)
Includes bibliographical references
and index
ISBN 0-8147-5190-3 (cloth: alk.
paper)
1. Nelson, Horatio Nelson,
Viscount, 1758–1805. 2. Great
Britain-History, Naval-18th
century. 3. Great Britain-History,
naval-19th century. 4 Great Britain.
Royal Navy-Biography. 5. Admirals-
Great Britain-Biography. I. Title. II.
Series.

DA87.1.N4L33 2003
359'.0092-dc21 2003042180
[B]

The British Library
HISTORIC LIVES SERIES:

Horatio Lord Nelson
Brian Lavery

Queen Elizabeth I
Susan Doran

26.00

Contents

'... I find myself again in command of the Mediterranean Fleet. I only hope that I may be able, in a small degree, to fulfill the expectations of my country.'

Introduction

Horatio Nelson was undoubtedly Britain's greatest naval leader, perhaps the greatest sea commander of all time. He was a superb seaman, an original and brave tactician and a charismatic leader. His character was complex and he made his share of mistakes and enemies, in both his public and his private life. His private life was confused, involving a passionate and adulterous affair with one of the most beautiful women of the age, and this only serves to make him more romantic in the popular imagination, while exposing his human fallibility. His death in battle in 1805 set the seal on his legend. Despite the fact that sea power and naval warfare are far less popular than they have been in past ages, Nelson can still be voted among the top ten Great Britons – against competition from people whose memories are far more recent.

Nelson's predecessors as sea commanders – Hawke, Boscawen, Rodney, Howe, Duncan and St Vincent – were highly successful admirals in their day and were heroes at the time, but today they are unknown except to specialists in naval history. His contemporaries and successors, including Collingwood, Ball, Saumarez, Troubridge, Hardy and Codrington, played a great part in the victories but they too are overshadowed by the great figure of Nelson. The men of the lower deck are largely forgotten except as victims of the press gang or as mutineers, although Nelson acknowledged that he could not have won his battles without their skill, determination and courage. On his column towering above Trafalgar Square in London, Nelson seems to dominate the naval history of the epoch, rather more than he did in reality. Nelson's epoch lives on in popular imagination in naval fiction, most famously written by Captain Marryat in the nineteenth century and by C.S. Forester and Patrick O'Brian in the twentieth. Although these novels give an excellent impression of life at sea, it is perhaps odd that Nelson hardly features at all in them, only as an off-stage character or, in one

Previous page: Nelson,
painted by Sir William Beechey, 1800.
National Portrait Gallery

Below: The *Boreas*, one of the many
ships in which Nelson sailed during his
distiguished and turbulent career.
National Maritime Museum, PAF5871

case, as a corpse. It is remarkable that fiction gives a slightly more balanced view
of naval history than popular history.

Attitudes to Nelson's faults have changed over the years. The twenty-first
century is not likely to make a great fuss about his adultery with Lady Hamilton,
but finds it less easy to forgive the cruel manner in which he broke off with his

wife. His persecution of the republicans of Naples, though justified by many of his biographers over the years, is deplored more than ever in an age in which democracy and nationalism are cherished. Yet Nelson's great qualities outweigh these faults. His charm and leadership impressed almost everyone he met. His seamanship, his ability to delegate and his eye for enemy weaknesses made him the victor of several great battles. And surprisingly, he eventually proved himself a successful administrator by running the Mediterranean Fleet for two years in difficult circumstances.

He can be compared with a more recent hero, Winston Churchill, who can also claim to have saved his country from invasion. Churchill's private life was blameless, but he made many political mistakes in his life, just as Nelson made tactical ones. Churchill lived a long and full life, but he was never one to avoid danger and, like Nelson, died amid outbursts of popular grief. Churchill was well aware of the role of his predecessor, and openly cried in front of a group of naval officers in 1941 when he watched the film *That Hamilton Woman*. If Churchill is the more famous of the two, it is mainly because he was the last great defender of his country.

Apart from the immediate results of his great battles, Nelson's legacy to Britain is complex. But his ideal of complete and uncompromising victory has survived the centuries and been a driving force for Royal Navy. The Second World War – with the heroism, patriotism and courage of its junior officers – irrefutably illustrates that Nelson's spirit endures, and perhaps it is most notably his spirit that continues to ensure him a place as one of Britain's greatest historic lives.

1

His father, Reverend Edmund Nelson, was a clergyman of thirty-five. He provided the young Horatio with one element which was always part of his character – he gave his son a lasting and sincere religious belief.

Early life and apprenticeship

On 29 September 1758 Catherine Nelson, wife of the rector of Burnham Thorpe in Norfolk, England, gave birth to a son. It was her sixth child, for two had died in infancy, while Maurice was now five years old, Susannah was three and William was nearly eighteen months. The boy was named Horatio, the same name as his late elder brother, and a compliment to his distant relative Horatio, Lord Walpole, but he was Horace to the immediate family. His father, Reverend Edmund Nelson, was a clergyman of thirty-five. He provided the young Horatio with one element which was always part of his character – he gave his son a lasting and sincere religious belief. As he grew older, the child showed another strong characteristic – unquenchable courage.

In 1919 Charles Davenport, a practitioner of the then popular science of eugenics, tried to prove that there was an hereditary element in great naval leaders, but Nelson caused him some difficulty. He had no direct naval ancestors, his brothers were generally undistinguished, feckless and even indolent, and Nelson's fearlessness and energy could only be explained by 'a dominant mutation'. The young Horatio soon had a reputation for initiative and daring. According to one legend recorded by his early biographers, he raided his headmaster's orchard when his schoolfellows were afraid; in another, his sister refused to stop a fight between him and his bullying elder brother. 'Let them alone, little Horace will beat him.' The boy once said to his grandmother, 'I never saw fear. What is it?'.

Nelson was born in the midst of the Seven Years' War, arguably the first real world war, in which armies battled for territory in Europe and for colonies in America and India, while navies fought in most of the oceans of the world. When the boy was born, the war was not going well. Minorca had been lost to the French, and Admiral Byng was shot as a scapegoat in 1757. The tide was beginning to turn by September 1758, and the boy's first full year of life, 1759,

C.
WIFE OF
BOR

Previous page: Catherine Suckling,
Horatio Nelson's mother, at the age of
eighteen, painted by J.T. Ileins.
National Maritime Museum, BHC 2879

was the famous 'year of victories' for the British when, according to Horace
Walpole the man of letters, 'Our bells are worn threadbare with ringing for
victories'. The last triumph of that year, the Battle of Quiberon Bay in
November, was the greatest British naval success so far. Horatio was only
four years old when the Treaty of Paris ended the war and gave Britain pre-
eminence in North America and India. He would have been precocious indeed
to understand it, but he must have been aware of the public rejoicing which a
great victory could bring to a remote corner of the British countryside.

The winter of 1767 was severe, and the vicarage at Burnham Thorpe was
never warm. Catherine Nelson was already worn out from eleven pregnancies,
including several which ended in miscarriages. She became sick, apparently
from pneumonia, and on Boxing Day she died. Reverend Edmund Nelson was
resigned – 'It has fallen my lot to take upon me the care and affection of a double
parent'. The young Horatio was the most vulnerable at nine years old. He now
lacked a mother figure, for his eldest sister Susannah, aged just twelve, was too
young to fill the gap.

His mother's untimely death gave Nelson a constant longing for female
attention and affection. Her passing, and his father's profession as a clergyman,
taught the young Nelson that life was transient and its death was never far away.
It helped to produce Nelson's well-known morbidity, but it also contributed to
his fearlessness for his own life, a valuable quality in a naval officer.

Horace's early education was in the Royal Grammar School at Norwich,
which took him away from home, but at least he had the comfort of a great-aunt
and a cousin in the town. At the age of eleven he moved with his brother to Sir
John Paston's School, North Walsham. He sat in a class of mixed ages, 'against the
wall, between the parlour door and the chimney'. He learned excellent literary

skills, and picked up a fair knowledge of Shakespeare, but 'Jemmy Moisson', the aged French master, failed to make him proficient in that language.

Although young Horatio's home was only three miles from the sea, there was nothing particularly maritime in his upbringing, and there are few anecdotes of him sailing from the Norfolk coast. His first contact with the Royal Navy was through his mother's brother, Maurice Suckling, who had entered the navy as a boy. In 1755, at the age of thirty, Suckling was promoted Captain. Two years later he was in command of the 60-gun ship *Dreadnought* in the West Indies where she and two other ships fought a spirited action against a larger French squadron, suffering thirty-nine casualties in the engagement. The date, 21 October, was celebrated 'as the happiest day of the year' among his family. After 1763 he was unemployed on half pay, like most naval officers in peacetime. He lived the life of a country gentleman at Woodton Hall, forty miles from the Nelson home at Burnham Thorpe.

Late in 1770 a dispute arose between Britain and Spain over the possession of the Falklands Islands and the British fleet was mobilised. It was a coincidence of great historical importance that Maurice Suckling was offered a ship, after seven years on shore and just as his nephew reached a suitable age to begin a seafaring career, for it was common for a young man to start at the age of twelve or thirteen in order to become 'inured to the hardships of a sea life', as a common phrase put it. This was an advantage to an impatient boy and it was twelve-year-old Horatio himself who suggested that he might go with Suckling. Captain Suckling commented, 'What has poor Horace done, who is so weak, that he, above all the rest, should be sent to rough it out at sea? But let him come and the first time we go into action a cannon-ball may knock off his head and provide for him at once.'

The parsonage house at Burnham
Thorpe, Norfolk, where Nelson was
brought up. The house was demolished
in 1802. Painting by Francis Pocock.
National Maritime Museum, BHC 1772

Suckling was wrong here. Nelson's appearance, and his apparent susceptibility to illness, suggested that he was frail, but his constitution was fundamentally very strong. The navy provided a suitable career for a spirited young man from a genteel but impoverished family. Little money was needed to launch a young officer in the navy, unlike the army, where commissions had to be purchased, or the law or the church in which expensive training was needed. In contrast, a young sea officer would learn on the job, and be paid for it. Suckling had no illusions about the hardships but Horatio was more than able to stand them.

Despite the fact that ancestry had always been considered important to a naval career, the navy expanded rapidly during each war of the eighteenth century, so many young men came in from outside traditional circles. As a career, the Royal Navy had certain attractions. It could accommodate the wildest sense of adventure and the most extensive wish to travel. It offered a unique chance to serve the king and gain honour, but at the same time to become rich through prize money from the capture of enemy warships and merchantmen. More than any other organisation of the time, it recognised merit among its officers.

Often young men were entered fictitiously on the books of a relative's ship to gain false sea time to advance their careers, but this did not happen with

Captain Maurice Suckling, Nelson's uncle, who arranged his entry to the navy and controlled his early career, making sure he had good training and appointments. Painting after Thomas Bardwell.
National Maritime Museum, BHC 3045

Nelson, perhaps because Maurice Suckling was ashore on half pay when it might have benefited his nephew. Nelson travelled south to join his uncle's ship at Chatham, Kent, in March 1771. He would have to undergo all the hardships of the naval service. Life was not always easy in the eighteenth century, even for sons of the middle class like Nelson, but the naval service was especially challenging. Horatio would have to live in a cramped berth below decks, with fourteen inches to sling his hammock and no privacy. At sea he might be on duty day and night for alternate four-hour periods. He would have to exist on salt meat and ships' biscuits, and eat them while the ship rolled in a gale. He had joined a service which was subject to fierce discipline, in theory at least. If he deserted or showed cowardice in action, he could be court-martialled and shot. As a potential officer he was not likely to be flogged publicly at the gangway like a common sailor, but he might be held over the barrel of a gun and caned – a practice known as 'kissing the gunner's daughter'.

There was a small Naval Academy at Portsmouth, but most people in the know regarded it as a waste of time. It certainly did not warrant missing the chance to serve under a captain who was also one's uncle. Nelson's training, as with the vast majority of officers and seamen of the day, was to be done on the job. There was little formal instruction except what the ship's officers might provide in their spare time. Nelson would have to learn to climb the rigging in a storm to take in sail, to make knots and splices, to row and to sail in a small boat, to steer the ship, to help operate the guns, to raise the anchors and to keep a look out. Later he would learn the extra skills needed by an officer – the technical ones of navigation, seamanship, gunnery and naval tactics, and the more personal ones of man-management and leadership. When he had mastered these, and had served for six years, he was entitled to sit a verbal examination for the King's commission as a lieutenant in the Royal Navy. After that he would have increased privileges – a cabin of his own, better pay and share of any prize money, half pay when there was no ship for him, as was common in peacetime, and the prospect of promotion to captain and eventually admiral.

But that seemed a long way away in March 1771 as Nelson approached his first ship. The young Nelson wandered round the naval port of Chatham, but no-one could direct him to his ship, until a kindly lieutenant took him in hand and had him rowed out to the *Raisonable* in a cold, biting wind. The ship was still largely unrigged and her guns had not been fitted; it took some effort of imagination to see her sailing and fighting. Maurice Suckling was absent, and it was the next day before he was able to greet his nephew. Nelson was only one of many people on board. The *Raisonable* had a total crew of 500 officers and men. She was allowed sixteen midshipmen, who in theory had served three years at sea before attaining the rank, and twenty captain's servants. Most of these were not domestics but boys, like Nelson, who were learning the trade with a view to becoming officers. Most ships had about eight midshipmen and captain's servants for every commissioned officer, so it was clear that not all the young men would make the grade. A few would die, and many more would drop out after a voyage or two.

If Nelson had joined his ship in wartime, he would have been thrust into a dangerous and bewildering world. He would perhaps have sailed straight away, and found himself in a terrifying naval action within weeks, before he could understand how to work, or even live, in the wooden world. This happened, for example, to Frederick Hoffman, who was later to serve under Nelson at Trafalgar, in the frigate *Blonde* in 1793. Instead, Nelson had a progressive education as a seaman and an officer, in an age when systematic training was not common. He started in the *Raisonable* in harbour, fitting out for sea, where he learnt the fundamentals of the trade – rigging and ropework. The threat of war with Spain was soon removed and the *Raisonable* did not put to sea, but Nelson was hungry for seafaring experience. He went on to a small merchant ship captained by a friend of his uncle for a return voyage to the West Indies. Like all merchant ships it was undermanned by naval standards and every man and boy had to pull his weight. He learned about the prejudice in the merchant service against the Royal Navy, for seamen were liable to be pressed into it in wartime. He learned to respect the men of the lower deck, and came away with the saying 'Aft the more honour, forward the better man' – for the officers lived towards the stern in all ships.

He returned to his uncle, now captain of the 74-gun *Triumph* at Chatham, but he had great difficulty in settling down again in a static guardship, moored permanently in harbour. Suckling encouraged him to learn navigation, holding out the reward that if he did so he would progress to the boats which the *Triumph*, like every other ship of the day, carried for various purposes. Nelson took every opportunity to get out in the ship's cutter and the longboat. He became a midshipman after fourteen months in the *Triumph*, with some authority over the crew, and took command of eight to twelve men, who would handle the boat under oars or sail, ferrying officers and crew to and from the shore and

The Medway in 1771, from a manuscript produced for King George III. The Royal Dockyard is in the left centre, beside the stretch of river marked 'Chatham Reach'. The lines across the river are mooring chains for ships 'laid up in ordinary', or held in reserve for future wars.
The British Library, Kings MS 44

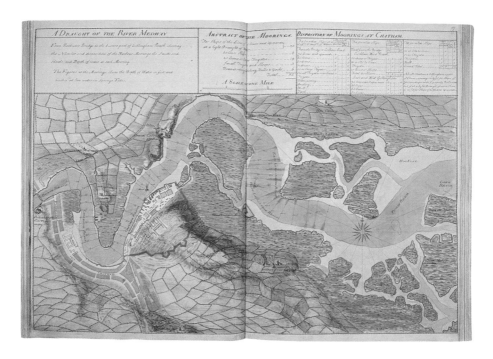

other ships, taking the captain up to London, and carrying small cargoes. The shallow waters of the Medway and Thames Estuary (the same rivers where Sir Francis Drake had learned his trade two centuries earlier) had many hazards, not all marked by buoys or beacons, and Nelson had a chance to concentrate on one kind of seamanship. In a biographical note he wrote, 'Thus by degrees I became a good pilot, for vessels of that description, from Chatham to the Tower of London, down the Swin, and the North Foreland; and confident of myself among rocks and sands, which has many times been of great comfort to me.'

The young Nelson fights off the attentions of a bear during his Arctic voyage, while the *Carcass* fires a shot to scare it off. The picture perhaps exaggerates the closeness of the bear and the danger he was in. From Clarke and Macarthur, *Life of Nelson*, 1809. *The British Library 1859 c5*

Although he began his naval career in peacetime, he was determined to expand his seafaring knowledge despite the lack of suitable appointments. He was prepared to drop in rank if necessary in order to stay at sea, even to posts which were technically lower deck and usually filled by ordinary seamen, not trainee officers – he had already served as a seaman on the voyage to the West Indies in 1772. In the summer of 1773 Nelson heard about a voyage of exploration in polar waters, to be led by Captains Constantine Phipps and Skeffington Lutwidge in the converted bomb vessels *Racehorse* and *Carcass*. Boys were banned from the voyage as being 'of no use', but Nelson cited his extensive experience of boatwork and managed to persuade Lutwidge to take him on as coxswain of the captain's barge, normally a lower deck appointment. While on the ice cap, Nelson hunted a polar bear to send the skin to his father, but his musket misfired. A crevice in the ice saved him, and the bear was scared off by a shot from the *Carcass*. Later in the summer, the ice floes began to close round the *Carcass* and her consort the *Racehorse*. Nelson was put in charge of a cutter and twelve men, and he played a significant part in navigating the ships through the ice.

Nelson returned to the *Triumph* after five months in the *Carcass*, but very quickly he heard of a warship going to the East Indies and applied to join it, as 'nothing less than such a distant voyage could in the least satisfy my desire for maritime knowledge'. He joined the 20-gun *Seahorse* under Captain Farmer and sailed east. During more than two years in the ship he got to know many ports in India, but he became seriously ill with malaria. He was sent home in the 20-gun *Dolphin* under Captain James Pigot, and on the way he had a quasi-religious experience. Lying on his sickbed he saw a 'radiant orb' and was filled with a sudden glow of patriotism. He vowed to himself: 'Well then, I will be a hero, and confiding in Providence, I will brave every danger.'

The plans of the *Dolphin* in the standard form of the period, showing, to the left, bow and stern views of the ship, with cross sections of the hull along its length. The side view, or sheer, of the ship, takes up most of the drawing. As well as external detail and gun ports it shows the positions of the decks and the ladders between them, with the steering wheel prominent near the stern. Below is a view from underneath, showing waterlines at various levels. *National Maritime Museum, 2683/42*

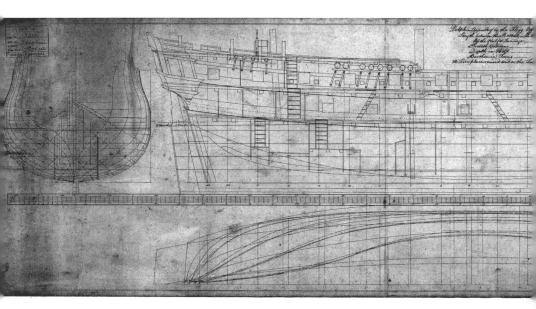

He returned to England in September 1776, to a changed situation. Conflict with the North American colonists had been developing for some years, and the latest news was of their Declaration of Independence from the mother country that July. The Americans had no fleet of their own, but they were using privateers to raid British commerce, and many more warships were put in commission to protect them. Nelson had not yet passed the examination for lieutenant, but on 24 September, just short of his eighteenth birthday, the Commander-in-Chief at Portsmouth offered him a great opportunity as acting lieutenant in the 64-gun ship *Worcester*. He spent the winter escorting convoys to and from Gibraltar, and was not daunted by his main duty as a lieutenant – taking charge of the ship during a watch of four hours, at any time of the day or night. Years later, he was

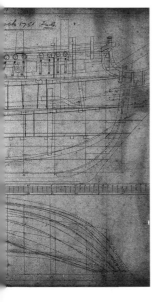

still proud that Captain Robinson had said of him that 'he felt as easy when I was upon deck, as any Officer in the ship'.

The lack of false sea time was probably just by chance, but somehow it symbolises the fact that there was nothing false about Nelson's abilities. He also had the fortune to serve under captains who took an interest in his training. On 5 April 1777, Nelson came before a committee of captains for an oral examination for full lieutenant, and his uncle still had a role to play. Suckling was now in a powerful administrative position as Controller of the Navy, and attended the board. He concealed his relationship with the candidate from the other captains and let Horatio do his best. After the captains had agreed that Nelson was fully worthy of a commission, Suckling introduced him as his nephew. By this time Nelson had done six years and three months at sea, and had thoroughly mastered the seaman's trade from the bottom up. He had never seen action, but his chance would come – the conflict with the American colonists was beginning to escalate into another world war.

The citizens of the thirteen colonies in North America objected to British taxation and revolted against British rule in 1775. In 1776 they declared their independence and a large British army had to be sent to America in an attempt to quell the revolt. The Americans had no navy, as such, but the British navy was needed to transport the British army from place to place and keep it supplied in hostile territory, to control American shipping and protect British trade from American raiders.

The character of the American War of
Independence altered when France
formed an alliance with the American
rebels, and Britain declared war early
in February 1778.

2

The American War

On 14 April 1777, five days after his examination, Nelson wrote one of the first
of his letters to survive. He told his elder brother William, a student at Cambridge
University, that he had attained his 'Degree as Master of Arts ... that is, passed the
Lieutenant's examination'. Nelson was a great letter writer, always lucid, frank and
engaging, giving considerable insight into the character of a man who had such
a great effect on world history. Perhaps the letters are not quite so revealing as
Pepys's diary, for example, but that was of course a secret document. Nelson was
rather less likely to reveal his innermost thoughts, his secret lusts, his frankest
opinions of his rivals, in letters than a diary. Sometimes he comes very close, but
there is inevitably a part of his inner self which he does not express.

Nelson's early career as a commissioned officer allowed him to continue his
learning of seamanship, and it was a formative experience in other ways. His first
appointment as a lieutenant was under a friend of his uncle's, Captain William
Locker, in the 32-gun frigate *Lowestoffe*. Locker was a humane, educated man
who was to remain a strong influence on Nelson for the rest of his life. The first
task was to get the *Lowestoffe* ready for sea, and in wartime that involved the press
gang, a crude form of conscription which consisted of taking up merchant
seaman, sometimes by force, and recruiting them to the Royal Navy. Nelson had
not encountered this directly before, but he saw the necessity of it, in the absence
of any better form of recruitment. He had the duty of conveying men between
the naval 'rendezvous' near the Tower of London to the *Lowestoffe* 50 miles down
river at the Nore, and it was during these trips that he visited the studio of the
artist John Rigaud to sit for a portrait that was to take many years to complete.

The *Lowestoffe* sailed for the West Indies in May and on 19 July she arrived
at the largest British island, Jamaica. It was Nelson's first trip to the Caribbean
since his service in a merchant ship as a boy six years earlier. The region was of

Cadiz Bay Feb.ʸ 20ᵗʰ 1777

Dear Brother

I write this from Cadiz were
we arrived on Saturday last after having
carry'd away our Main Yard in Kings.
I am very Sorry that I could not see Charles
Boyles but your letter & the Parcel from
Mʳ Robertson I sent in the Zephyr Sloop
as the most Expeditious way as the
Enterprize is expected at Mahon very
Soon, & will not be at Gibralter before
next May, Charles bears an exceeding
good Caracter & is much beloved in
the Garrison of Gibralter, when you
write to my Father let him know you
heard from me I have wrote to the Compt.ʸ
by the Same post but weither you will
receive this before my arrival in England
I know not. but I shall come to town

Previous page: Nelson's first known
letter to his brother February 1777, in
which he writes that he has attained his
'Degree as Master of Arts... that is,
passed the Lieutenant's examination.'
The British Library, Additional MS 34988, f.1

great economic importance to the western European powers, for its sugar
plantations, worked by black slaves, produced enormous profits which helped fuel
the war machines. In wartime, islands changed hands with surprising frequency,
and if powers like France and Spain were to enter the war on the side of the
American colonists, the region would become a main centre of conflict. In the
meantime, American privateers were raiding the area, and American merchant
ships were carrying out illegal trade. In October the *Lowestoffe* chased an American
privateer and the crew surrendered, but it was difficult to board her in a heavy sea,
for a boat had to be sent across. The first lieutenant tried and failed and Locker
asked, 'Have I no Officer in the Ship who can board the Prize?'. The master was
about to get into the boat, but Nelson, as second lieutenant, was next in line. 'It is
my turn now; and if I come back, it is yours.' Nelson's grounding in boatwork
stood him in good stead – he was almost washed aboard the American ship by a
large wave but eventually he got on board and took the prize to Jamaica.

However, as Nelson himself put it, 'even a frigate was not sufficiently active
for my mind.' The *Lowestoffe* captured a small schooner and Locker decided it to
use it in support of the frigate. He named it *Little Lucy* after his eldest daughter
and gave the command to Nelson. It was not the same as the independent
command of a ship, which is what Nelson most desired, but it was more than
a ship's boat and it aided Nelson's development in more ways than one. 'In this
vessel I made myself a complete pilot for all the passages through the (Keys)
Islands situated on the north side Hispaniola' – a vital area for stopping enemy
trade, and one of the most complex navigations in the world. This was entirely
typical of the two years which Nelson spent as a lieutenant or acting lieutenant.
He was constantly gaining new experience and building on old skills, while
maintaining a high degree of independence from central control.

Nelson steps into a boat in very rough seas to board and take possession of an American privateer. From Clarke and Macarthur, *Life of Nelson*, 1809.
The British Library 1859 c5

The character of the American War of Independence altered when France formed an alliance with the American rebels, and Britain declared war early in February 1778. Nelson was transferred to become third lieutenant of the 50-gun *Bristol*, under Vice-Admiral Sir Peter Parker. Service as a junior officer in a relatively large ship was clearly very different from what he had been used to, and might be seen as a severe blow to his independence, despite the prestige of serving in the flagship. But it had a very real advantage. The commander-in-chief of an overseas station, like the West Indies, had the power to promote his subordinates to commander or even captain without reference to the Board of Admiralty. Naturally he would choose those under his own eye, particularly the lieutenants in his flagship. Captain Suckling died in July that year and Nelson wrote, 'He did not forget me, but recommended me in the strongest manner to Sir Peter Parker whose [sic] has promised me he will make me the First Captain.'

Apart from this period and his early apprenticeship in the *Raisonable* and *Triumph*, when he spent most of his time in the ship's boats, and a short time in the *Worcester*, Nelson had never served as a junior officer in large ship. It could be a dispiriting experience, particularly when long periods were spent at anchorages such as Spithead or Torbay, in England, or in long cruises off blockaded ports. It was a life of 'uniform sameness, day after day, and month after month', as Nelson later discovered. He spent little time in wardrooms, where a dozen or so junior officers might have to live together for years. The seamen lived in messes, and one of their very few privileges was to change mess on giving notice to the first lieutenant. Officers, however, were stuck together in the wardroom with no chance to move. Small differences between them were magnified, and disputes and personal feuds were common. The standard method of advancement was to accumulate enough seniority to become first lieutenant of a ship, and then be promoted to commander after the ship distinguished herself in action. In the meantime, many officers became absorbed in ship administration.

Nelson by-passed this by fast promotion. He rose quickly and was first lieutenant of the *Bristol* by September, as the officers above him were promoted. In December, after less than a year in the *Bristol*, he was promoted commander and took charge of the tiny brig *Badger*. Thus he avoided the factionalism, the excessive concern with seniority and the bureaucracy that was common among naval officers of the age. Nelson never became deeply involved in the administrative tasks of a junior commissioned officer of the day, so he was never obsessed with organisation, as some officers became. This did not mean that he was a poor administrator, as his running of the Mediterranean Fleet from 1803–5 shows. Even more important, he had no completely unhappy experiences in his early years. Nothing happened to take the edge off his enthusiasm for the naval service and throughout his life he maintained the charm, the zeal, the openness and the imagination of a newly joined midshipman. It is no surprise that he spent much of his time with the midshipmen when he was in command of a ship or a fleet, rather than with the more embittered senior officers.

Little is known for certain about the *Badger*, except that she was very small, but she was probably an American prize commissioned into the navy. Nelson was ordered to take her to the Mosquito Coast of Honduras, to protect the area from American privateers. He made friends with the rough diamonds who had settled

Nelson's letter on hearing of the death of his uncle in 1778.
The British Library, Additional MS 34988, f.4

there, but had much worse relations with merchant shipping. He sent a press gang on board some merchant ships, with orders not to press men if the ships were homeward bound. Five men were brought in from a ship called the *Amity Hall* against instructions, and Nelson intended to send them back, when the master of the merchantman came on board and addressed him 'in a most impertinent manner, and with very abusive language'. Nelson sent three men back but kept two 'for his impertinent behaviour'. The affair was reported to the admiral, and Captain Locker was uneasy about Nelson's role in it.

But Nelson continued to be highly active and courageous, as would be the pattern for the rest of his career, with an embarrassment quickly followed by a success. In June the *Badger* was anchored in Montego Bay, Jamaica, close to the 20-gun *Glasgow*, when the latter ship caught fire. Nelson used the boats of the *Badger* to rescue some of the crew and prevent damage to other ships in the anchorage.

Nelson's command of the *Badger* did not last very long, and the brig's captain changed so rapidly that one suspects Parker used it as a device to give his protégées some sea time as commander before further promotion. On 11 June 1779, Nelson got the vital promotion to captain of the 28-gun *Hinchinbrook*, a small frigate recently captured from the French.

At the early age of twenty years and eight months, Nelson was a full, or post-captain in the Royal Navy, the most successful fighting service of the age. He ranked with a lieutenant-colonel in the army, the commander of a regiment of 1,000 men. In seniority, he was at the bottom of the captain's list, but he would rise through it and in the end, after fifteen to twenty years, he would be promoted to rear-admiral (the most junior grade of admiral, or 'flag officer'). In the meantime, he had enormous powers and responsibilities. The lives of 200 men were in his hands, and he could flog any seaman, disrate any petty officer and send any officer or man to a court martial which might apply the supreme penalty of death. In wartime he could send out press gangs to take merchant seamen into the navy. He was responsible for the safety of the vessel in rocks and storms, for her safe navigation, for carrying out the duties required by admirals and senior captains, and for directing the ship in action with the enemy. Expectations of naval captains were high and failure was not tolerated; though Nelson was driven on by his internal ambitions, rather than any fear of punishment.

Britain and France had been at war since 1778, after the British army's defeat by the Americans at Saratoga in 1777 had caused France to sign an alliance with the American rebels. In the meantime Nelson had to wait for his new ship to arrive at Jamaica, and he observed how the island was 'turned upside down' by the threat of invasion, for the French Admiral D'Estaing had arrived in the West Indies with a large fleet, the first of several which would enter the Caribbean during this war. Nelson took command of some of the batteries for the defence of the capital, Port Royal, but by the time the *Hinchinbrook* arrived the hurricane season had begun, and it was October before he set sail as a post-captain. He had some success, capturing four enemy merchant ships in company with two other frigates, and shared in £800 prize money.

He was 'the merest boy of a Captain I ever beheld', dressed in a quaint and old-fashioned uniform. 'I had never seen anything like it', wrote the Prince, but as with many others, the first impressions soon proved mistaken.

In June 1779 Spain had entered the arena and declared war on Britain, hoping to recover British-held Gibraltar and Florida. This created a large combined Franco-Spanish fleet which outnumbered the Royal Navy in the English Channel and threatened invasion that summer. It also opened up the prospect of British action against the vast and apparently vulnerable Spanish Empire in Latin America. Strategists noticed how narrow the isthmus of Panama was; how the navigable San Juan River led to Lake Nicaragua, whose western shore was only eleven miles from the Pacific. It revived a long-standing dream of a new route to the east, to vast wealth. An expedition was prepared, and Nelson was chosen to command the naval part of it. He visited the army commander, Colonel Polson, who wrote, 'a light-haired boy came to see me in a little frigate, of whom at first I made little account'.

There were delays, and the best season was missed. It was the end of March 1780 when the *Hinchinbrook* anchored near the mouth of the San Juan River, with a strange group of ship's boats and native canoes, manned by soldiers, sailors, irregular militia and native Indians. The river had not been navigated since the times of the Spanish buccaneers, so local pilots were rare and ill-informed. Some boats had to be left behind, as the crews were exhausted from carrying the others over shallows or rapids. At the first Spanish fort, Nelson led his men in 'boarding' the enemy. On 10 April they reached the larger castle of San Juan, 100 miles up river and Nelson set up batteries to bombard it, but before the Spanish surrendered at the end of April, Nelson was appointed to another ship and left; the British and their allies were too exhausted and ill to exploit the victory. Out of the *Hinchinbrook's* complement of 200 men, eighty-seven were sick and the forces were withdrawn. Nelson fought against illness, but eventually he too succumbed to malaria, dysentery and exhaustion and had to return to Jamaica to recover.

The Rigaud portrait of Nelson, as finally completed in 1781, showing a young and very thin captain after his experiences in Nicaragua.
National Maritime Museum, BHC 2901

Nelson's next ship was the 44-gun *Janus*, bringing a substantial increase in status and pay, but he was still in poor health and he resigned the command to sail home that autumn in the *Lion*, under Captain William Cornwallis. In the meantime Admiral Rodney had arrived in the West Indies with a large part of the British battlefleet. He fought three actions with the French in April and May, but Nelson played no part in them.

Nelson arrived in England in December and stayed with his friend Locker in London before going to Bath to meet his father. His condition was no better and an expensive physician, Dr Woodward, was hired to treat him. He was in considerable pain, had to be carried to and from bed, and some of his limbs were paralysed. Woodward prescribed regular baths in the hot springs and Nelson began to recover slowly. He left in March 1781, visited his brother in London and went back to his family in Norfolk. The portrait by Rigaud was now completed with the castle of San Juan in the background, and Nelson's appearance and uniform updated. Early in August, after a year out of service, he was offered the command of the frigate *Albemarle*. By

this time the war in America was going badly; General Cornwallis had been surrounded by American troops and French naval forces at Yorktown, and he would be forced to surrender with almost 8,000 men in October.

The *Albemarle* was a captured French merchantman and Captain Locker was highly critical of her suitability as a warship, but Nelson was defensive. He first saw her in dry-dock at Woolwich and was pleased with her underwater lines. 'She has a bold entrance, and clean run.' He was allowed to choose his own officers and when the ship's company was assembled he considered them 'as good a set of men as I ever saw'. The ship was slow in fitting out and winds were unhelpful, so it was late in December before she reached the anchorage at Great Yarmouth, not far from Nelson's home, to begin duty in escorting convoys of merchant ships against the Dutch (who had joined the war in 1780). Again Nelson had missed a fleet battle, for on 5 August, just before he took command of the *Albemarle*, the Dutch and British fleets had fought it out at Dogger Bank. On 26 January 1782 the ship was in the Downs, off the coast of Kent, when a tremendous gale struck. While Nelson was ashore, an East India store ship dragged her anchors and was driven into the *Albemarle*. At first the local boatmen refused to row Nelson out to his ship, until an offer of fifteen guineas ($£15.75$) brought a rush of business. She lost her foremast and bowsprit, and her lightly built structure was weakened.

After the surrender at Yorktown the British mostly gave up hope of recapturing the American colonies, but they had some success when they took Dutch possessions in the West Indies and India. The centre of the war now shifted to the West Indies, where the main force of the British and French fleets was massed. After repair at Portsmouth, the *Albemarle* was ordered to escort a convoy to Quebec, though she had not been improved by the accident and Nelson wished for 'a better Ship and a better station'. Once in North America he was sent on a 'cruise' against enemy shipping, with a good chance to make a fortune from prize money. He captured and destroyed a number of ships, 'more … than is seldom done in the same space of time', but regarded it as a failure, because none of the prizes made it back to port where they would be sold. Off Boston he was chased by a squadron of three large French ships and a captured British frigate, and was in danger of being taken. He led them over the shallows of St Georges Bank, which was enough to deter the ships of the line, but the frigate, much larger than the *Albemarle*, continued to gain on him. By sunset she was almost within gunshot range, and Nelson ordered the *Albemarle's* main topsail to be backed, stopping the ship in the water and offering battle. The Frenchman declined and headed back to his squadron.

At New York in November, Nelson met another officer who was to have much influence on his life. Prince William, third son of King George III, was serving as a midshipman and recorded his first impression of Nelson. He was 'the merest boy of a Captain I ever beheld', dressed in a quaint and old-fashioned uniform. 'I had never seen anything like it', wrote the Prince, but as with many others, the first impressions soon proved mistaken. 'There was something irresistibly pleasing in his address and conversation; and an enthusiasm, when speaking on professional subjects, that showed he was no common being.'

Nelson was at last with the main fleet under Lord Hood and sailed with it to the West Indies. The biggest British victory of the American War of Independence had already been won in April that year while Nelson was on the way to Quebec, when Admiral Rodney defeated a substantial French fleet off the Saintes in the West Indies. Hood's force too was battle-hardened, having twice fought the French Admiral De Grasse in 1781–82. Nelson now longed for similar action, and according to Prince William he was indifferent to prize money and wanted to command a ship of the line. Nelson admired Hood, and this was reciprocated. 'He treats me as if I was his son, and will, I am convinced, give me anything I can ask of him.' In March 1783 Nelson was sent to help recapture Turk's Island from the French, but news arrived that peace had been concluded in January, with the British possessions in the West Indies still intact. The fleet was ordered home and the *Albemarle* arrived at Portsmouth on 25 June, with orders to pay off the crew.

Nelson's career in this period was remarkable in that he spent very little time with the main fleet, which took up most of the officers and ships. Partly this was because his genius for independent command had already been noticed; but more often he was just unlucky to be out of service when the main battles were taking place in that theatre. But he had enjoyed a rapid rise for such a young man, and had gained experience in many kinds of seamanship and warfare. Though he complained that he had 'closed the war without a fortune', Nelson had done remarkably well in other respects.

'Her personal accomplishments you
will suppose I think equal to any
person's I ever saw; but, without
vanity, her mental accomplishments
are superior to most people's of
either sex ...'

Peacetime and marriage

In the summer of 1783 Nelson claimed he had seen enough of sea service for
now and wrote to Captain Locker, 'I have no thought of going to sea, for
I cannot afford to live on board ship, in such manner as is going on at present'.
In July he took up residence in Salisbury Street, off the Strand in London, where
he suffered another bout of illness. In October he applied for six months leave of
absence in France, for he knew that knowledge of the language was 'a very useful
and necessary part of a sailor's education'. He travelled with his friend Captain
James Macnamara, who had served with him in the *Bristol* five years earlier.

Like many an English tourist before and since, Nelson was amazed and
largely unimpressed by French customs. The roads were cobbled and the carriages
had no springs, so the two officers were 'pretty well shook together' after a day's
journey. His inn was 'a pigstye' where he was fed on pigeons and slept on straw.
Six years before the French Revolution, he noted the great gulf between classes.
At Montreuil 'there are no middling class of people: sixty noblemen's families
lived in the town, who owned the vast plain round it, and the rest very poor
indeed.' He found Boulogne to be full of Englishmen, 'I suppose because wine is
so very cheap' but in other places he found no-one with enough knowledge of
English to teach him French.

Arriving at St Omer he was pleased to find it 'a large City, well paved, good
streets, and well lighted'. He found good lodgings, where the landlord's daughters
provided some incentive to learn their language. The two captains tried to keep
away from the numerous English families in the area, for visiting them would
undermine the purpose of their trip. In particular they avoided Captains Ball and
Shepherd of the Royal Navy, for they had affected gold epaulettes on their
uniforms, not officially approved by the Royal Navy until twelve years later –
they were 'coxcombs', 'a little *cheap* for putting on any part of a Frenchman's

Previous page: Frances Nelson, née
Nisbet, drawn by Daniel Orme in 1798,
eleven years after her wedding.
National Maritime Museum, A94

uniform'. Nelson took much interest in Miss Elizabeth Andrews, the daughter of
an English clergyman and wrote in some distress to his uncle William Sucking,
hoping for an increase in his allowance to facilitate his marriage to a lady 'of a
good family and connexions but with a small fortune'; instruction in French
proceeded 'but slowly'. In January 1784, disappointed in his pursuit of Miss
Andrews and grieving for the recent death of his sister Anne, Nelson returned to
London. Intending to rejoin Macnamara in France after a few weeks, he settled
back in Salisbury Street and found that 'London has so many charms that a man's
time is wholly taken up'.

By March 1784, Nelson was delighted to be appointed to the frigate *Boreas*
of 28 guns. When his brother William asked him what 'interest' he had used to get
such a rare peacetime appointment he replied proudly, 'having served with credit
was my recommendation to Lord Howe, First Lord of the Admiralty'. He would
have preferred the East Indies, but Nelson soon found out that he was to serve in
the Leeward Islands, in the West Indies. He appointed his brother William as the
ship's chaplain.

The voyage of the *Boreas* was unlucky from the start. On the way out of the
Medway an incompetent pilot ran the ship aground on a falling tide, and she was
left high and dry 'with so little water that people could walk round her' until the
next high tide – an intense humiliation for Nelson, who always prided himself
on his navigation. At anchor off the Downs he had a dispute with a Dutch East
Indiaman and his conduct was reported to the Admiralty, who backed him up.
He went ashore at Portsmouth but had an accident when he had to throw
himself off a runaway horse.

In May, the *Boreas* sailed from Spithead, carrying a large number of passengers.
There were three women – Lady Hughes, the wife of the admiral on the station, her

daughter, and the ship's purser's wife – as well as about thirty midshipmen going out to join their ships. Nelson did not get on with Lady Hughes and her daughter. He tired of her ladyship's 'eternal clack' and wrote of her daughter with uncharacteristic sarcasm, 'What a specimen of English beauty'. When they left he wrote 'I had rather have their room than their company.' Yet Lady Hughes was the first to notice one of the outstanding characteristics of Nelson's style of command – his unique concern to educate and encourage his midshipmen. She noted 'His attention to the young gentlemen who had the happiness of being on his Quarter-deck. It may reasonably be supposed that among the number of thirty, there must be timid as well as bold; the timid he never rebuked, but always wished to show them he desired nothing of them that he would not instantly do himself.' Nelson would challenge them to a race to the masthead, and make light of its dangers. He would visit them in the extemporised school-room, and join them in calculating the noon position of the ship. 'How wise and kind in such a proceeding!' exclaimed Lady Hughes.

Nelson arrived at Barbados, the most important island in the area, at the end of June. He was the senior captain, under Rear-Admiral Hughes, but he was friendless and unhappy during September, when he was confined to Antigua during the hurricane season. His brother left due to bad health and although the admiral was 'tolerable' as a commander, Nelson did not like him, and avoided his wife as much as possible. His friend Captain Cuthbert Collingwood was at Grenada, some distance away and his only support was Mrs Moutray, wife of the Commissioner of the dockyard at Antigua, who was 'very, very good' to him. She became a 'dear sweet friend' and only the presence of her husband prevented a full love affair from developing. This did not prevent Nelson having a professional difference with her husband, the first of many disputes. Moutray, though a captain on half pay, was actually employed as a civilian official and had no right to give

The *Boreas* off a West Indian island,
drawn by Nicholas Pocock.
National Maritime Museum, PAF 5871

orders to naval captains in command of ships. Nelson made sure that he, and the
Admiralty, knew this.

The British islands – Barbados, Antigua, Dominica, Nevis, St Kitts and several
others, were of considerable economic importance. Sugar was grown there by slave
labour and sold at vast profit in Britain and Europe. The islands were constantly
fought over, and St Lucia, recently returned to French control, changed hands
fourteen times in 150 years. The French, Spanish and Dutch each still maintained
a strong presence in the region. During his first year, Nelson went to the well-
sheltered port of English Harbour, Antigua, at the end of July to lay up for the
hurricane season, leaving in November to get bread in Barbados, as supplies
were short on other islands. After that he did some surveying in the Virgin Islands
and by January 1785 he was in Basse Terre Roads, St Kitts, with orders to patrol
Monserrat, Nevis, Anguilla and the Virgin Islands. He was back in English Harbour
in February for repairs and at Barbados again by the middle of the month.

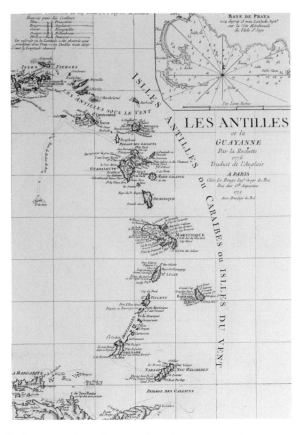

The islands of the Lesser Antilles as drawn by Thomas Jefferys and published in 1775. *The British Library, 118 f 14*

According to James Wallis his first lieutenant, 'He never suffered the ship to remain longer than 3 or 4 days in any island at a time. She was always on the wing, and when it happened that any of the other ships were in company, he was always forming the line, exercising, chasing etc.' He was back on his station at St Kitts by mid-March and carried out patrols before spending the next hurricane season in English Harbour, where he exercised the midshipmen in music, dancing and fighting with cudgels, while the officers staged plays to keep themselves occupied.

Nelson soon found a cause worthy of his attention. The Americans had declared their independence of the British Empire, and had just fought a major war to prove the point; yet their ships were still to be found in large numbers among the British islands, carrying out much of the trade. This was a clear breach of the Navigation Acts, which decreed that British colonies could only trade by means of British ships. Yet no-one, from the admiral and the colonial governors downwards, seemed to care. To Nelson it was not just a technical breach of the law. The object of the Navigation Acts was to encourage the growth of British shipping, providing a pool of seamen for the navy. As he wrote in 1786, 'This traffic … will increase the ship-building of America, and raise the numbers of her seamen; while, on the contrary, it will decrease the British Shipping and Seamen in these Islands.' But it went much further than that. The islanders, in his opinion, were close to the Americans in culture and economics, 'as great rebels as ever were in America' and only deterred by British seapower. The Americans, he believed 'will first become the Carriers, and next have possession of our Islands, are we ever again embroiled in a French war.' Nelson began a campaign, almost single-handed, against the American trade with the British islands. It is ironic that Nelson, who originated the phrase after losing the sight of one eye in 1794, was the only one who could not turn a blind eye to the situation.

Admiral Hughes reluctantly gave Nelson permission to put a stop to the American trade in November, but the Governor of the islands, Major-General Thomas Shirley, was more obstructive. In March 1785 he wrote to Nelson, 'old and respectable officers of high rank, long service and a certain life are very jealous of being dictated to in their duty by young gentlemen whose service and experience do not entitle them to it.' Nelson replied audaciously that he was the same age as William Pitt the Prime Minister, and that he 'thought himself as capable of commanding one of H.M. ships as he was of governing the state'.

Matters came to a head and on 2 May Nelson seized the schooner *Eclipse* of Philadelphia then on 23 May, off Nevis, he took four American ships with false papers. The ships were soon condemned as smugglers in the court on Nevis, with Nelson eloquently pleading his own case, but then their captains sued him for £4,000. They claimed that they had been detained aboard the *Boreas*, guarded by a sentry brandishing a sword, and forced into confessing that they were Americans. In fact the sentry was the marine who guarded the captain's cabin in any warship, but Nelson was not sure of his ability to defend himself in court with public opinion running against him. He was unable to leave the safe haven of his ship for five months for fear of a writ being served on him, except on

Nelson replied audaciously that he
was the same age as William Pitt the
Prime Minister, and that he 'thought
himself as capable of commanding
one of H.M. ships as he was of
governing the state'.

Sundays. When his first lieutenant suggested that his situation was to be pitied,
Nelson replied, 'I hate pity. I shall live to be envied and to that point I shall
always direct my course.' Nelson had no support from his admiral but he wrote
to the King and to Lord Sydney, the Home Secretary, who eventually agreed to
support him in court. But four years later, Nelson was still trying to get prize
money for the four ships from the Collector of Customs at Nevis.

There was one positive result from Nelson's isolation, at least in the short
and medium term. President Herbert of Nevis was the only official to back him,
and Nelson spent considerable time at his residence on the island. His first
appearance there early in 1785 was unimpressive as he arrived 'much heated, and
very silent', and remained taciturn throughout the meal, despite heavy drinking.
A fellow guest observed, 'there was such a reserve and sternness in his behaviour
with occasional sallies, though very transient, of a superior mind.' Six months later
he was back, and this rather forbidding character was found playing with a child
under the dining-room table.

The boy was the five-year-old Josiah Nisbet, and Nelson soon came to
know his mother Frances. She was the same age as Nelson, the niece of the
President and widow of a surgeon. Nelson quickly developed great affection
for the quiet, intelligent woman, a contrast to the 'clack' of Lady Hughes. In June
1785 he wrote cryptically that within a month he might become 'a Benedict'
or newly married man. Things did not develop quite as fast as that, but by
September 1785 he was writing regularly to Frances when away from Nevis,
and in November he announced his intentions to his cousin William Suckling.
He might smile and say 'This Horatio is for ever in love', but Nelson assured
him that the present attachment was of 'pretty long standing'. 'Her personal
accomplishments you will suppose *I think* equal to any person's I ever saw; but,

without vanity, her mental accomplishments are superior to most people's of either sex; and we shall come together as two persons most sincerely attached to each other from friendship.' To James Wallis, first lieutenant of the *Boreas*, she was 'beautiful and amiable'.

In July 1786 Admiral Hughes struck his flag and gave up the command. Nelson, a captain of seven years standing, became the senior officer on the Leeward Islands station. This was a remarkable opportunity for a twenty-seven-year-old officer, though perhaps it was part of a policy of appointing young men to commands to give them practical experience in peacetime. When five captains were assembled to preside over a court martial in 1787, Nelson was the oldest at twenty-eight, followed by Captain Holloway at twenty-six, Captain Newcombe at twenty-five, and Prince William Henry and Commander Wilfred Collingwood, both twenty-two. His brother Cuthbert Collingwood, a long-standing friend of Nelson's, had left in 1786, aged thirty-six.

In December 1786 Nelson was joined by his new captain, His Royal Highness Prince William Henry, third son of King George and eventually king himself. Nelson was pleased to have royalty under his command and participated in numerous balls held in William's honour. But all was not well in William's ship, the *Pegasus*. The Prince was a fierce disciplinarian and insisted that his men wear blue uniforms, long before naval uniform was officially adopted for the lower deck. His first lieutenant, Isaac Schomberg, took the liberty of allowing the men to take off their blue jackets in warm weather, and this led to an open dispute with the Prince. Nelson backed the Prince and Schomberg was put under arrest before being sent home. Several of the Prince's men were court-martialled, including the master at arms who ought to be a figure of authority on any ship, and the Prince was constantly in dispute with his midshipmen. Nelson continued

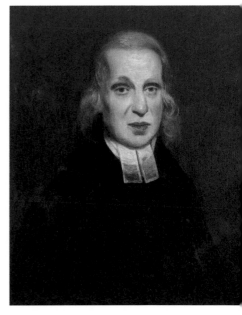

to back him up in disciplinary matters, but he was treading on more dangerous ground when the Prince failed to provide a muster book as required by the dockyard authorities. This brought Nelson into conflict with the Navy Board in London, a dangerous position for a relatively junior officer, and when he tried to root out corruption in the dockyard at Antigua he made more enemies. In April 1787, when seaman William Clark was court-martialled for desertion from the sloop *Rattler* and sentenced to death, Nelson accepted Prince William's advice to pardon him – waiting, as was customary, until the rope was actually round the man's neck before announcing it. The Admiralty later pointed out that pardons were the prerogative of the King, and Nelson only had authority to suspend the sentence. Just as bad from the Admiralty's point of view, Nelson had discharged Clark from the navy without authority.

After some delays due to operational necessities, Nelson married Frances Nisbet on Nevis on 12 March 1787, and Prince William gave the bride away. The day after the wedding his friend Captain Thomas Pringle recognised Nelson's potential, despite the various troublesome situations he had been in. He was expressing a common attitude when he observed that 'the Navy lost yesterday its greatest ornament by Nelson's marriage. It's a national loss that such an officer should marry. Had it not been for that circumstance I foresee he would be the greatest officer in the service.' His command in the West Indies was coming to an end, and the *Boreas* was in poor condition and had to leave before the next hurricane season. Nelson sailed from Nevis in May and his wife travelled separately in a merchant ship. The *Boreas* arrived at Spithead in July and Captain Nelson went on half pay.

After some time in London and Bath, Horatio and Frances went to Burnham Thorpe to see his father, not planning to stay. He had been forced to rely on his wife's skills to entertain French officers in the West Indies, so he planned to go back to complete his learning of the language. But on arrival in Norfolk, the welcome was effusive, and the old clergyman was so cheered up by the visit that the couple settled there. Nelson wrote: 'In short this good old man seemed to suffer much at the thought of us leaving him, saying his age and infirmities were increasing and that he could not last long which made us give up entirely our former plan. Then we agreed to live together. A great convenience to Mr N. and some convenience to all parties.'

Nelson settled into a routine at Burnham Thorpe. He took up gardening and began to farm his father's glebe, sometimes digging with great energy to tire himself out. He read the newspapers, partly to look for opportunities to revive his career – no war meant limited military postings – but he had few literary interests. After 1789 he watched the events of the French Revolution with horror, and supported the local Norfolk magistrates against clubs which advocated revolution there; at the same time he was sympathetic to the plight of poor farm labourers. He visited London occasionally to collect his half pay and to lobby for appointments, and once a year he visited Lord Walpole, and his relative Coke of Holkam, the famous agricultural improver. Still he could not shake off the legal problems of the Leeward Islands command, and in 1790, while Nelson

Nelson began to look at other careers outside the British navy and at one stage he considered applying for service in the Russian navy, where many British officers made good in the eighteenth century.

was buying a horse at a fair, Mrs Nelson was served with notification of an action by the owners of two American vessels. He was defended by the Crown, and it came to nothing. His finances were shaky: his half pay was just over £100 per year, and his prize money from previous campaigns seems to have been dissipated. In June 1791 his current account had a balance of £7.0.4 [£7.02] and six months later this had fallen to just £1.2.0 [£1.10]. He bought a ticket in 'Shergold's Chance', a lottery or sweepstake, but won nothing.

Nelson began to look at other careers outside the British navy and at one stage he considered applying for service in the Russian navy, where many British officers made good in the eighteenth century. By the early 1790s he was thoroughly dissatisfied and according to Frances, would never have gone to sea again 'if he had had a fortune'. As he did not, he continued to look out for national events which might aid his chances for sea employment. When a new Board of Admiralty was appointed in 1788, he wrote indicating his 'readiness to serve'. The fleet was mobilised in 1790, on a passing threat of war with Spain. A squadron under his old commander Lord Hood was fitted out. Prince William, now the Duke of Clarence, was given the command of a ship of the line but Nelson was not, a situation he found 'most mortifying'. He appealed in person to Hood and was told, in perhaps the most crushing moment of his naval career, that 'the King was impressed with an unfavourable opinion of me'. He did no better in 1791, when the fleet was raised again on a threat of war with Russia.

However, at the beginning of 1793 everything changed. War with revolutionary France was imminent, and Nelson was offered the command of his first ship of the line, the 64-gun *Agamemnon*. He wrote in his delight, 'After clouds comes sunshine. The Admiralty so smile on me, that I really am as much surprised as when they frowned.'

45

4

'My ship is, without exception, the finest 64 in the service, and has the character of sailing most remarkably well'

The Mediterranean Campaign

Some captains would have spurned the command of the *Agamemnon*, for 64-gun ships, with only 24-pounder guns as the main armament, were rapidly becoming obsolete. They were the smallest type of 'ship of the line', so-called because they were (only just) large enough to stand in the line of battle against the strongest opponent. In 1795 it was reported that 'There is no difference of opinion respecting 64-gun ships being struck out of the rates. It is a fact that our naval officers either pray or swear against being appointed to serve on board them.' But Nelson was in love with the ship from the first. In February, even before he had put to sea, he wrote to his brother, 'my ship is, without exception, the finest 64 in the service, and has the character of sailing most remarkably well'. He was not disillusioned with her in practice, and after several months at sea he still regarded her as 'a fast sailer'. This might be put down to elation at his first command of a ship of the line, of his delight at being back at sea again after a long and fretful period on shore, and being back in favour at the Admiralty. But his love for the ship continued long beyond that honeymoon, and he declined to be transferred to a larger and more suitable 74-gun ship on several occasions.

After a few cruises with the Channel Fleet, which Nelson regarded as futile, the *Agamemnon* was sent to the Mediterranean under Admiral Hood, now very much restored in Nelson's estimation. The Mediterranean was important in British strategy, not because it offered great prospects of trade and colonies, but because of the need to control the French fleet at Toulon, which might break out into the Atlantic, dominate Italy or move eastwards to threaten the British in India. It was also important because it helped the British to link up with actual or potential allies such as the powerful state of Austria–Hungary.

In August it seemed that British supremacy in the area would be confirmed, when the French Royalists allowed allied armies to enter the great naval base at

The RIGHT HON.ble   EARL of St. VINCENT

Knight of the Most   Hon.ble Order of the Bat.

Admiral of the   White Squadron

Pub.d by Bunney & Gold, Shoe Lane 1. August. 1800.

Previous page: Admiral Sir John Jervis, who took command of the Mediterranean Fleet on 30 November 1795. Jervis said of Nelson, his 'zeal, activity and enterprise cannot be surpassed'.
The British Library, The Naval Chronicle, *vol IV*

Toulon. Nelson's role was to maintain relations with allies in the area, using the good sailing qualities of the *Agamemnon*. He was sent to make contact with the governments of Turin and Naples, to ask for 10,000 troops to help in the occupation. He was impressed with the dramatic scenery of the latter port and wrote, 'nothing could be finer than the view of Mount Vesuvius'. He was even more impressed on meeting the British Ambassador, Sir William Hamilton, and his beautiful wife Emma. Everyone knew of her humble background as a former servant, and there were rumours of a more scandalous life as a prostitute. Despite this Nelson found her 'a young woman of amiable manners, and who does honour to the station to which she is raised.'

But the Toulon campaign was a failure. The allied troops of the various nations could not work together and a young artillery major, Napoleon Bonaparte, led the counter-attack for the revolutionary government. The allies withdrew and Captain Sir Sidney Smith was given the job of burning the enemy ships in the Toulon base, which he failed to do effectively. 'Great talkers do the least', Nelson wrote of the talented but boastful Smith.

On 22 October Nelson had his first encounter with the French afloat in this war, when the *Agamemnon* met a force of three frigates and two smaller ships. Seriously undermanned, she suffered some damage to her rigging and limped into a Sardinian port for repairs.

It was not long before Nelson was deeply involved in the next campaign. Pascal Paoli, a veteran nationalist, had declared Corsica's independence from France in April 1793. In the first days of 1794 Admiral Hood concluded an agreement with him; the French would be driven from their remaining positions, mostly in the fortresses of the island, and it would then become subject to the British crown. A British force of sixty ships set out to land in St Florent Bay, but

was dispersed by storms. Meanwhile Nelson raided round the north of the island, destroying a water mill which he believed to be essential to French supplies and capturing or destroying sixteen supply vessels. He carried out a reconnaissance on Bastia, the capital of the island, noting that the French defences were becoming stronger; the British army thought it too dangerous to attack, and the navy had to do it alone. Nelson blockaded Bastia in the *Agamemnon* until 4 April, when Hood began his attack on the town. Nelson had another crucial role, in command of the ships' guns which were landed to bombard the fortified town from the shore side, while the rest of Hood's fleet formed a ring to attack from seaward. He describes the work; 'From April 4th to the 10th, all the Seamen were employed in making batteries and roads, and in getting up guns; works of great labour for so small a number of men ...'. New batteries were opened over the weeks, but Nelson found he could not get close enough to do real damage. The siege lasted forty-one days

The western Mediterranean in 1794,
published by Laurie and Whittle,
contemporary map-makers whose products
were used by many naval officers.
The British Library, Maps 146 cl (26)

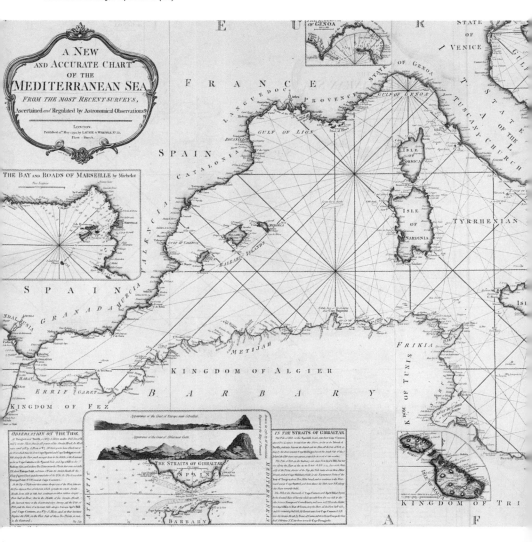

until the French surrendered and during this time Nelson's stepson Josiah Nisbet, now a naval lieutenant, distinguished himself, as did Lieutenant George Andrews, whose sister Nelson had unsuccessfully courted at St Omer.

Having shown some skill in amphibious operations, Nelson was now put in charge of the naval side of the siege of Calvi, in the north-west shoulder of Corsica. He arrived with sailors and troops on 19 June and the British landed numerous heavy guns, including seven from Hood's flagship, the *Victory*, but the citadel was strongly defended and ready for a long siege.

On 12 July, while Nelson was directing the fire of the batteries, a shot hit a sandbag near him and sent splinters of pebbles towards him. One fragment hit him near the right eye and at first he made light of it. It was 'a little hurt', 'a very slight scratch', and he was more worried about the cosmetic effects. However, there was some loss of vision, which he eventually realised was permanent, and he could only distinguish light and dark with that eye. A month later it was 'nearly deprived of its sight'. Six months later he wrote, 'My eye is grown worse, and is in almost total darkness, and very painful at times; but never mind, I can see very well with the other.' It seems that he had suffered a concussive injury, possibly to the retina. The superficial wounds soon healed and, contrary to popular misconception, he never wore a patch over the eye. The siege of Calvi lasted 51 days, until the French surrendered on 10 August.

To Nelson's regret, Lord Hood went home in October due to ill health, and in May 1795 he was removed for speaking out on the inadequacy of force in the Mediterranean. Command devolved on Vice-Admiral William Hotham, a typically cautious officer of the old school – who according to Nelson had 'no head for enterprise, perfectly satisfied that each month passes without any losses on our side'.

By 1795, now aged thirty-seven, Nelson was a vastly experienced officer, having taken part in many kinds of activities – exploration, patrol, convoy escort, skirmishing and amphibious warfare. At the end of the year he claimed to have been in more than 140 fights in two wars. But until May 1795 he had never taken part in a fully-fledged single ship action against an enemy ship of equal force, or in a major fleet battle, regarded as the real test of a navy and its men. For more than a century, fleet tactics had been dominated by the line of battle, in which all the major ships were drawn up in a single line to get the maximum effect from their gunfire. In practice it was a clumsy and largely defensive arrangement, and if both sides used it there was little chance of a decisive victory. Since the 1740s the more adventurous admirals had been finding ways to move away from this type of battle.

It was remarkable that Nelson had still spent hardly any time with the main fleet. In the American War he had commanded frigates on detached service. After a few years' service an average captain would be promoted to command a ship of the line, which brought more pay but less prize money. But in peacetime few ships of the line were fitted out because of the expense, and after 1783 Nelson was perfectly happy to remain in frigates. During his time of unemployment he had missed the mobilisations, when the ships had been drilled in fleet manoeuvres. And more recently, though technically part of the main battlefleet, he had spent nearly all his time on detached service at Naples and Corsica. As a result, Nelson had never been drilled in the tight discipline of a battlefleet. His independent mind had never been tamed by the need to practice forming a line of battle, turning in succession, sailing on a line of bearing and all the other routines of formal battle. He never had to break out of any tactical strait jacket, for the simple reason that he had never been in one. Uniquely, Nelson came to fleet battle with great nautical skill but no tactical preconceptions.

> Nelson wrote to his wife, 'had we taken ten sail, and allowed the 11th to escape when it had been possible to have got at her, I could never have called it well done'. This was the credo for the rest of his life.

Nelson had his first taste of battle when the Mediterranean Fleet met the French off Corsica in March 1795. He was almost the only captain to engage the enemy seriously, rushing ahead in a general chase to attack the damaged *Ca Ira*. He turned his ship occasionally to fire broadsides from as little as 100 yards into her stern, resulting in her capture, along with another 74-gun ship which attempted to tow her. Hotham stopped the pursuit and Nelson went on board the flagship in a great rage. Hotham replied coolly that, 'We must be contented. We have done very well.' The nation was satisfied with this, and Hotham was voted the thanks of both houses of Parliament, but Nelson wrote to his wife, 'had we taken ten sail, and allowed the 11th to escape when it had been possible to have got at her, I could never have called it well done'. This was the credo for the rest of his life.

The fleets met again on 13 July, with even less effect. Again there was a chase, and Nelson tried to get the *Agamemnon* alongside a French 80-gun ship; but the wind died away then came from a different direction, allowing the French to escape. One French ship was captured and blew up. Nelson was not dissatisfied with Hotham's leadership this time and concluded, 'I will say no ships could behave better than ours, none worse than the French'.

The war in Europe did not go well for British during 1795, as her allies withdrew from the campaign. The Netherlands, Belgium and Luxemburg were taken over by the French while Spain and Prussia made peace. There was stalemate in Northern Italy, where Austria engaged with France among the patchwork of states there. Nelson spent the last months of the year in charge of a small squadron off the coast of Italy in support of Austrian armies. It was a frustrating experience, in which he sometimes found himself 'in the cleft stick'. In December he had to stay at Genoa to rescue retreating troops, rather than going to Pietra to deal with enemy gunboats harassing the Austrian left flank. The campaign convinced him 'by ocular demonstration, of the futility of Continental Alliances'.

On 30 November, Admiral Sir John Jervis arrived to take command of the Mediterranean Fleet. He was 'a perfect stranger' to Nelson but he soon proved himself a commander to his taste. By February he was writing of 'Captain Nelson whose zeal, activity and enterprise cannot be surpassed.' The relationship remained a long-distance one, for Nelson was off the coast of Italy for the first half of 1796, while Jervis was with the main fleet off Corsica and Toulon. Nelson was rather cocky. 'Opportunities have been frequently offered me, not only as a gallant man, but having a head; for, of the numerous plans I have laid, not one has failed, nor of the opinions given, has one been in the event wrong.' He was promoted commodore, a temporary rank between captain and admiral. A fellow captain summarised his career. 'You did just as you pleased in Lord Hood's time, the same in Admiral Hotham's, and now again with Sir John Jervis!'

Jervis was keen that Nelson should stay under his command, a slightly ironic compliment for one who professed to long for home, and he wrote to Fanny postponing their joint dream of 'a cottage of our own, and an ample income to live on'. By now the condition of the *Agamemnon* was causing concern, and in June Nelson feared that she would not be fit for another winter without major work in a home dockyard. Reluctantly he transferred to HMS *Captain*, the first of several 74-gun ships he would command over the next few years. The 74 was the classic ship of the line. With only two gundecks it was too small to support the dignity of a senior admiral, but it had good sailing qualities and a heavy gun armament, and formed the bulk of every major battle fleet.

Nelson had great expectations for British rule in Corsica, finding it a beautiful place, a possible centre for British trade in the Mediterranean and a naval

base for controlling the French in Toulon. He hoped it might develop under British rule in the same way as Ireland, an unfortunate example considering that the latter island was soon to fall into a vicious circle of revolt and repression.

For British supremacy in the Mediterranean, 1796 was a bad year. In the spring and summer Napoleon Bonaparte led his armies against the Austrians and defeated them in northern Italy, forcing them out of the war; and in August, France and Spain signed an agreement which was likely to lead to war between Britain and Spain. On 25 September Jervis wrote to Nelson that Corsica was to be evacuated, as the position was likely to be cut off. Nelson accepted this in his official letters but he was more frank to his wife – the evacuation was 'a measure which I cannot approve. They at home do not know what this fleet is capable of performing; anything, and everything.' Nelson was equally sure that the Spanish navy was not a real threat. He had high regard for the honour of its officers, but the experiences of them as allies at Toulon had only highlighted their weaknesses. In a few months' time he would have a chance to show how right he was.

In the meantime he was given the job of evacuating the British from the capital, Bastia. There was chaos ashore as the loyalty of the Corsicans shifted in the face of British abandonment and the French army's advance. Nelson threatened to use the guns of his ships if the local people hindered his evacuation, and that seemed to work. Ships' boats worked by day and night for four days taking off 'cannon, powder, stores, and provisions, exclusive of baggage, household stuff, &c., &c.'. He was last to leave the beach early in the morning of 20 October, after the French had already taken the citadel. He had no sympathy with the Corsican dilemma in the face of what they might interpret as a British betrayal. 'Now, John Corse, follow the natural bent of your detestable character, plunder and revenge.' By the end of the month he was off to Gibraltar in the *Captain*, and the British fleet had virtually withdrawn from the Mediterranean.

One task remained, and that was entrusted to Nelson. The British garrison of the island of Elba, a few miles off the Italian coast, was still in place and Jervis wanted to evacuate it to avoid being cut off. On 15 December he sailed from Gibraltar in the frigate *La Minerve*, with the frigate *Blanche* under his command. Four days later, off the Spanish port of Cartagena, they encountered two Spanish frigates in the darkness. *La Minerve* captured the Spanish *Sabina* after nearly three hours of action, with seven of her men killed, while the *Blanche* took the other. The captured ship was taken in tow, a British prize crew went on board and the Spanish captain and officers were transferred to *La Minerve*. But at 4.30 that morning, a Spanish frigate came up and fired a broadside into the prize, which had to be cast off. A Spanish ship of the line and another frigate surrounded *La Minerve*, and the *Blanche* was too far away to windward to help. Even Nelson had to admit failure in the circumstances. He was thankful that they 'very narrowly escaped visiting a Spanish prison'.

The two frigates reached Elba on 27 December, and Nelson landed to find a ball in progress at the house of the governor, General de Burgh. Nelson was delighted when the band struck up 'See, the Conquering Hero Comes' but the general felt he had no authority to evacuate the island, and a month was spent in

'Opportunities have been frequently offered me, not only as a gallant man, but having a head; for, of the numerous plans I have laid, not one has failed, nor of the opinions given, has one been in the event wrong.'

indecision. The frigates sailed on 29 January 1797, carrying naval stores as well as Nelson's friend Sir Gilbert Elliot, the late Viceroy of Corsica. Nelson did a reconnaissance in the Toulon area then dropped Elliot at Gibraltar. He then proceeded to join St Vincent's fleet, now off Cadiz in Spain where its object was 'the defence of Portugal, and keeping in the Mediterranean the Combined Fleets' (of France and Spain).

On leaving Gibraltar, *La Minerve* was again pursued by a superior Spanish force, of two ships of the line. One of them was gaining on the frigate when a man fell overboard. Lieutenant Thomas Hardy, recently released from Spanish captivity, set out in the jolly-boat to try to rescue him, and was in danger of being carried towards the enemy and renewed imprisonment when Nelson called out 'By God, I'll not lose Hardy: back the mizzen topsail'. The frigate's speed was reduced and the boat's crew was picked up. Fortuitously, the leading enemy ship mistook their actions as a direct challenge, and slowed down to await her consort, allowing *La Minerve* to escape.

The ship was still not safe and during the night she found herself in the middle of a Spanish fleet, but again she was able to escape. On 13 February Nelson finally rejoined Jervis off Cadiz. He reported the presence of the Spanish, and then returned to his own ship, the *Captain*. He had little time to reflect on the total British failure in the Mediterranean – from a position of almost absolute dominance, the Royal Navy had now withdrawn completely from a sea that was regarded as essential to the British strategy of containing the French by sea and defeating them by land with the aid of allies. Nelson might have taken consolation from the fact that the failures were nearly all military and diplomatic, as it was the lack of allies in the area, and the enmity of Spain, which forced the withdrawal, rather than any naval failure.

5

St Vincent and Tenerife

The fleet which Nelson had passed through was the Spanish one commanded by Admiral Cordoba, escorting a valuable convoy of mercury into Cadiz, and for once Nelson was lucky in that he had arrived just in time for a full-scale battle. On hearing of their position, Admiral Jervis prepared his fleet for action, drawing them up in two parallel lines. Soon after dawn on 14 February the Spanish were sighted in some disorder, with the main force some distance from a smaller group of ships of the line and transports. Jervis headed for the gap and at 11 a.m. he put the fleet into line of battle 'as most convenient', allowing the faster ships to go the head. Nelson, in the *Captain*, remained near the rear of the line however. The British had fifteen ships of the line, the Spanish had twenty-seven, some much larger than the British ships, but the Spaniards were poorly manned and commanded by inexperienced officers. The ships of the main Spanish force turned and began to head north towards Cadiz, and the British fleet passed between them and their convoy. In order to keep his line intact Jervis ordered his own ships to tack in succession, each turning when it reached a certain point, so that the leading ones at least would catch up with the sternmost ships of the enemy, but the process was slow and there was a danger that the bulk of the Spanish fleet might escape.

In the *Captain* towards the rear of the line, Nelson was the first to spot this danger, and that there was a far quicker route to the enemy. He anticipated his orders when he wore his ship round and headed straight for the largest ships of the Spanish fleet, though in fact Jervis noticed the same point a few minutes later and made signal which allowed it. The *Excellent* under Captain Collingwood, at the rear of the line, also turned to support Nelson, while at the other end of the line the *Culloden* under Captain Thomas Troubridge was just coming into action. There was soon an apparently unequal contest between this small group of three

Previous page: Nelson in the *Captain* attacks and boards the *San Nicolas* and *San Josef*, painted by Nicholas Pocock and engraved by J. Fittler. From Clarke and Macarthur, *Life of Nelson*, 1809. The British Library, 1859 c5, vol 1

74-gun ships and a group of six or seven Spanish ships, including the *Santisima Trinidad* of 130 guns, at least two more three-deckers, an 80-gun ship and several 74s. The *Captain* was dismasted and lost her steering wheel, but Nelson was undaunted and with great panache he led his men in boarding the *San Nicolas*, leaping through the window of a quarter gallery which had been broken by a soldier. 'I found the cabin doors fastened and some Spanish Officers fired their pistols; but having broke open the doors, the soldiers fired and the Spanish Brigadier (Commodore with a Distinguishing Pendant) fell, as retreating to the quarter-deck on the larboard side, near the wheel. Having pushed on the quarter-deck, I found Captain Berry in possession of the poop, and the Spanish ensign hauling down. I passed with my people and Lieutenant Pierson on the larboard gangway to the forecastle, where I met two or three Spanish Officers prisoners to my seamen, and delivered me their swords.'

Not satisfied with this, Nelson then boarded the *San Josef* which was alongside the prize. The Spanish, already battered by Nelson's guns, soon surrendered and the officers handed over their swords on the quarterdeck. Nelson gave them to Seaman William Fearney of his barge crew, who put them under his arm 'with the greatest sangfroid'. After the exploit, it was dubbed 'Nelson's patent bridge for boarding first rates' in the fleet.

Nelson's actions had created a major victory, at a time when national morale was severely depressed. In all, four Spanish ships were taken, with few losses on the British side. Nelson himself was bruised on the stomach, but 'not obliged to quit the deck'. Jervis was made a peer, taking his title, the Earl of St Vincent from the site of the battle. Nelson had already been promoted to rear-admiral, though he did not know it until afterwards and Frances, on hearing an account of the battle, urged him in future to leave the boarding to captains. Although he was

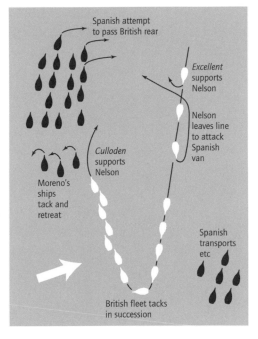

The Battle of St Vincent, showing the British ships in white. The main body of the British fleet has sailed between the Spanish warships and their convoy, and forms a v-shape as they tack to come up on the rear of the enemy battlefleet. To the top right, Nelson turns out to make a faster approach to the enemy, followed by the *Excellent* under Collingwood.

Spanish attempt to pass British rear

Excellent supports Nelson

Nelson leaves line to attack Spanish van

Culloden supports Nelson

Moreno's ships tack and retreat

Spanish transports etc

British fleet tacks in succession

knighted, Nelson's role was under-stated in the official dispatch, perhaps because Jervis was persuaded not to give too much praise to a man who had anticipated his orders. The situation was reversed, however, later in the year when Colonel John Drinkwater, an eye-witness to the battle, published an account giving Nelson due prominence and Nelson became a public figure and a national hero in Britain for the first time.

The British position in Europe and the Mediterranean continued to decline. General Napoleon Bonaparte defeated the Austrians decisively in northern Italy and forced them to withdraw from the war with large territorial losses. Britain was now left with only one ally, Portugal, and there was no decisive way of getting at the French. Politicians considered the possibility of peace but, in the meantime, the navy had to do its job, despite dissatisfaction among the seamen.

St Vincent's fleet now set up a very tight blockade of the port of Cadiz, trapping the remainder of the Spanish ships. Nelson wrote that 'We are looking at the ladies walking the walls and Mall of Cadiz.' Meanwhile there was mutiny in the fleets at home, and a serious danger that it might spread to St Vincent's fleet as well, despite the admiral's vigilance and repression. In May Nelson shifted

Opposite: Santa Cruz de Tenerife from
three miles east in 1791.
The British Library, The Naval Chronicle,
vol XIV

his rear-admiral's flag to another 74, the *Theseus,* taking Captain Miller and some
of the officers of the *Captain* with him. The discipline of his new ship was 'an
abomination', caused by a discontented crew and lax officers. After two weeks
of reform, a note signed by the ship's company was found on the quarterdeck.
'Success attend Admiral Nelson God bless Captain Miller we thank them for the
officers they have placed over us. We are happy and comfortable and will shed
every drop of blood in our veins to support them, and the name of the *Theseus*
shall be immortalised as high as the *Captain's.*'

As the French consolidated their power in the Mediterranean, the British
tried to contain the enemy forces outside that sea. Early in July Nelson led a
direct, but unsuccessful, attack on the Spanish position at Cadiz. A bomb vessel,
the *Thunder,* was brought in to fire explosive shells onto the town, supported by
a small gunboat from Gibraltar. Numerous ships' boats took to the water to form
a screen as the *Thunder* bombarded the fort of San Sebastian. Spanish gunboats
and barges came out in defence and there was fierce hand-to-hand fighting. The
coxswain of Nelson's barge, John Sykes, saved him twice from Spanish swords.
Sykes, though a common seaman, was singled out by Nelson – 'his manners and
conduct are so entirely above his station, that Nature certainly intended him for
a gentleman.' He tried to have him promoted lieutenant, but he had not served
long enough to qualify.

The Royal Navy had a constant dream of capturing a Spanish treasure
ship when it was bringing several million pounds worth of gold back from her
colonies. In one stroke, the participants would become fabulously rich, the rest
of the fleet would be given an incentive, and the Spanish economy would be
seriously damaged. In April 1797 there were already rumours of such ships
sheltering in the harbour at Santa Cruz on Tenerife, and Nelson drew up a

detailed scheme to invade and bombard the island and capture them. 'My plan could not fail of success, would immortalise the undertakers, ruin Spain and has every prospect of raising our Country to a higher pitch of wealth than she has ever attained.'

The plan called for 4,000 troops, but the army refused to support it. Nelson was not surprised, having seen the army's caution and incompetence in Corsica. Anticipating St Vincent's later view that the army should be disbanded and the country defended by an expanded marine corps, he decided to proceed with a smaller force of marines. Meanwhile, two Spanish ships were actually discovered sheltering at Santa Cruz, and two frigates were able to capture the less valuable one, from Mauritius. The Manila galleon, the *San Jose*, remained, holding a cargo believed to be worth several hundred thousand pounds. Convinced of the value of the attack (and no doubt aware that the commander-in-chief was entitled to an eighth of that sum), St Vincent gave Nelson three of his best 74-gun ships, three frigates and two smaller vessels, and their captains included Ralph Miller, Thomas Troubridge, Samuel Hood and Thomas Fremantle who had served with Nelson before, and gained his admiration.

The force left the main fleet on 15 June and headed slowly south in light breezes. Four conferences were held to settle the plans in detail. Nelson, in overall command, did not intend to land himself. On 21 July parties of seamen and marines from each ship were assembled in the frigates. That night the frigates towed the ships' boats as close inshore as they could, they were cast off and headed for a beach between the town and the Castle of Paso Alto. Progress was slower than expected in unfavourable winds, the Spanish were alerted and fired on the force, and Thomas Troubridge ordered a retreat. It was decided to try another plan – to land further away from the town and send men up to the heights above it to dominate it and the castle. They got ashore and exhausted themselves in the summer heat by climbing one hill, only to find that a deep valley separated them from where they wanted to be. Again the force retreated and by this time the men of the *Theseus* had apparently reverted to type – they were 'the most tiresome, noisy, mutinous people in the world'.

Nelson got intelligence from a German deserter from the Spanish army, that the 'The Spaniards have no force, are in the greatest alarm, all crying and trembling, and that nothing could be easier than to take the place.' The previous attempts had evidently failed because of Troubridge's panic and poor navigation in the hills. Nelson held a council of war with his captain and decided on a more direct attack, which he would lead in person. They would land on the seafront of the town itself and Nelson's own party would attack the breakwater near the centre of the town, protected by the Castle of San Cristobal and by a battery on its end. Other parties led by Troubridge, Miller and Hood would land further south.

The landing force of just over a thousand men set off before midnight on 24 July, covered by fire from the hopefully-named bomb vessel *Terror*. As the boats approached the shore the Spanish opened a devastating fire, for the town was defended by 1,669 men, not 300. The boats were put into confusion and many failed to land. Nelson's barge beached and the men began to disembark. The admiral was in the stern awaiting his turn when a Spanish musket shot hit Nelson in the arm. He fell back with the words 'I am shot through the elbow'. His

> In a sense he was already what history remembers him as – a one-eyed, one-armed admiral highly successful in battle, a charismatic leader and a popular hero. But the greatest phase of his life had not yet begun.

stepson Lieutenant Josiah Nisbet was by his side and had the presence of mind to apply a tourniquet.

Nelson was rowed back to the *Theseus*, having refused to be taken aboard the frigate *Seahorse* for fear of alarming Captain Fremantle's wife who happened to be on board. He was taken below to the cockpit where Surgeon Eshelby and his two mates decided to amputate above the elbow. Nelson put on a brave face as usual, but felt the full pain as the cold knife cut away the flesh.

In the meantime, the British forces which had landed were surrounded. Samuel Hood managed to persuade the Spaniards that they could burn the town unless they were allowed good terms. They were allowed to leave with full military honours and keep their weapons, but had to promise not to attack the town again. Nelson had generally been successful in land operations up to now, particularly at the long sieges of Bastia and Calvi. The Tenerife operation was very different in character, depending on speed and daring – what we might call, in retrospect, more Nelsonian. But Nelson's appreciation of enemy weakness, while very accurate on the sea, did not apply to the land. Both the French and Spanish were strong on their own element.

If the loss of Nelson's eye was underestimated at the time, and the stomach injury at St Vincent was hardly mentioned, there was no mistaking the nature of this wound. It was traumatic in every sense of the term. Nelson took the pen in his left hand for the first time and wrote to St Vincent, with pain and uncertainty in every letter:

> *I am become a burthen to my friends, and useless to my Country; … When I leave my command, I become dead to the World; I go hence, to be no more seen. … I hope you will be able to give me a frigate, to convey the remains of my carcase to England.*

y will be able to give me a frigate to convey th[e]
remains of my carcase to England, God B[less]
you My Dear Sir & Believe Me your
Most obliged & faithful
Horatio Nelson

You will excuse My Scrawl
considering it is my first Attempt —

Sir John Jervis K B.th

Three weeks later, he was no more cheerful; 'A left-handed admiral will never
again be considered as useful, and therefore the sooner I get to a very humble
cottage the better, and make room for a better man to serve the State.' To his
wife he was no more optimistic – '... I shall not be surprised to be neglected
and forgot, as probably I shall no longer be considered as useful.' He was still in
considerable pain, for one of the ligatures had apparently been gathered up with
a nerve or sinew. He could feel 'ghost' pains in his arm, and with characteristic
faith he considered this to be proof of life after death.

Nelson's spirits began to recover after he arrived in England on 1 September.
He was lauded as a national hero for his role in the St Vincent battle, and Lady
Nelson nursed him back to health, in perhaps the happiest period of their
marriage. Together they bought a cottage at Roundwood, a 'modern built
messuage' near Ipswich, fulfilling a long-standing dream and giving Nelson a
home of his own for the first, and in a sense the only, time in his life. In London
Nelson met the First Lord of the Admiralty, Earl Spencer, and charmed his wife.
At first she thought him 'a most uncouth creature' with the appearance 'of an
idiot', and no doubt his recent traumas had not improved his looks. But once in
conversation, 'his wonderful mind broke forth'. Early in December he placed a
paper in St George's Church in London requesting a prayer of thanksgiving. 'An
officer desires to return thanks to Almighty God for his perfect recovery from a
severe wound ...' and within a few days he was pronounced fit for service. In a
sense he was already what history remembers him as – a one-eyed, one-armed
admiral highly successful in battle, a charismatic leader and a popular hero. But
the greatest phase of his life had not yet begun.

Spencer and St Vincent were agreed about one thing – that Nelson, with his great determination and his extensive knowledge of the western Mediterranean, was the man to lead the expedition.

The Nile Campaign

By now, after beating the Spanish navy at St Vincent and the Dutch at Camperdown, the British were victorious at sea (except in the Mediterranean) and the French armies carried all before them on the continent of Europe. It was difficult to see how one side could finally defeat the other in the circumstances. Off Cadiz, Admiral St Vincent resisted attempts to make him take his fleet back into the Mediterranean. The politicians in London could see that the war against France would never be won by sea power alone and desperately needed an ally, especially Austria which had the best army in Europe apart from the French. A fleet in the Mediterranean would link up with them and reassure them about British intentions. By the end of March 1798 a new factor was beginning to emerge. Newspapers, reports from consuls in neutral countries and spies all concurred that something unusual was happening at Toulon. French and Italian merchant ships were being requisitioned in large numbers, troops were marching there, and it soon emerged that the rising star of the French army, General Bonaparte, was going there to lead them. Urged on by Earl Spencer at the Admiralty, St Vincent accepted that at least a small force would have to be sent to Toulon to see what was going on.

Spencer and St Vincent were agreed about one thing – that Nelson, with his great determination and his extensive knowledge of the western Mediterranean, was the man to lead the expedition. At first Sir Horatio was offered a fine new ship, the 80-gun *Foudroyant*, but her completion was delayed. Nelson got another 74, the ten-year-old *Vanguard*, with his newly promoted friend Edward Berry as flag captain. He left most of the work of fitting out the ship to Berry, as was proper, but he went to a good deal of trouble to secure his own men as officers. He took an unprecedented step in using Edward Galwey as his first lieutenant, though Nathaniel Vassal was senior to him. 'If they do not

choose to stand as I like in my ship, they may stay away; and so I have told Mr Vassal.' Michael Jefferson, formerly of the *Agamemnon*, was the surgeon, while the midshipmen's berth included several relatives and family friends from Norfolk. His servant Tom Allen of Burnham Thorpe came too, as he did on many of Nelson's voyages, but he had rather an ambiguous regard for him. According to one officer he was 'clumsy, ill-formed, illiterate and vulgar ... but his bold heart made up for all his deficiencies and ... Tom Allen possessed the greatest influence with his heroic master.'

Berry brought the ship round from Chatham, where she was fitted out, and Nelson joined her at anchor in Spithead on 29 March. As he unpacked his trunk in the great cabin he was unable to find some of his clothing and wrote petulantly to Frances, 'I have looked over my linen, and find it very different to your list, as follows...'. A little later he wrote, 'My place is tolerably comfortable, but I do not shine in servants.'

The *Vanguard* sailed on 1 April and a month later Nelson joined the fleet off Cadiz. He went on board St Vincent's flagship to an effusive welcome. He was given his orders – 'to proceed ... up the Mediterranean and endeavour to ascertain by every means in your power, either upon the coast of Provence or Genoa, the object of the equipment.' He was to be given two 74s in addition to the *Vanguard*, and three frigates to reconnoitre and take messages back to the main fleet. The force assembled at Gibraltar and Nelson was reunited with an old friend, Captain Sir James Saumarez of the *Orion*. Less welcome was Alexander Ball, captain of the other 74, the *Alexander*. Nelson had last encountered him fifteen years before at St Omer, when he despised him for wearing epaulettes. Nelson now said to him, 'What, are you come to have your bones broken?' Ball, humourless as always, replied that 'he certainly had no wish to have his bones

The dismasted *Vanguard* being towed to safety by the *Alexander* (with detail on page 69), drawn by Nicholas Pocock. The *Vanguard* suffered extensive damage from a gale on 20 May 1798. *National Maritime Museum, PW 5876*

broken, unless his duty to his King and country required such a sacrifice, and then they should not be spared.'

The six ships sailed on 8 May, and were off Toulon ten days later. Nelson was pleased with himself. He 'had his squadron about him, who looked up to their chief to lead them to glory, and in whom the chief placed the firmest reliance, that the proudest ships in equal numbers belonging to France would have bowed their flags ...'

Disaster struck in the evening of Sunday the 20th, in the form of a gale from the north. The *Vanguard* was hardest hit. At 1.30 in the morning her main topmast, crowded with men taking in sail, broke and fell over the side, but most of the men managed to scramble back on board. The mizzen topmast followed and then the whole of the foremast broke, damaging the bowsprit. The ship was being driven inexorably towards the rocky coast of Corsica, until Nelson was able to turn her using what scraps of sails were left. The other two 74s, *Orion* and *Alexander*, were relatively undamaged by the gale and stayed close to the flagship, but the three frigates were separated and never found Nelson again until the campaign was over.

The wind did not moderate until the 22nd, by which time the three ships of the line were close to Sardinia, and the *Vanguard* was in danger of drifting onto the coast. The *Alexander* took her in tow, but the winds dropped almost to nothing and the danger of drifting increased, so Nelson ordered Ball to cast it off. Ball refused, and in one moment he gained Nelson's undying respect. He showed seamanship, courage, and a willingness to disobey orders when he knew he was right. The three ships made it to the small harbour of San Pietro in the south of

Sardinia, where much of the *Vanguard's* rigging was repaired, though she had a stumpy foremast for the rest of the campaign. Nelson never dreamed of abandoning his mission by going to the British base at Gibraltar for repair.

There had been further developments in London. Spencer found ten more 74-gun ships to join Nelson and sent them on to St Vincent under the command of Captain Thomas Troubridge. Nelson got back to his station off Toulon on 3 June, to see nothing of his missing frigates. But there was great joy on the 5th when contact was made with the tiny British brig *Mutine* under Captain Hardy, travelling in advance of Troubridge's ships. The combined force, of thirteen 74-gun ships and two smaller vessels, was now 'a match for any hostile fleet in the Mediterranean'. But Bonaparte's fleet had already sailed on 20 May, missing the local storm which had done so much damage to Nelson.

Nelson sailed for neutral Naples, where his friend Sir William Hamilton was ambassador. Troubridge went ashore and was back two hours later, with news that the French had gone to Malta. Nelson took the fleet through the Straits of Messina and on the morning of 22 June, just east of Sicily, two events occurred in quick succession. Captain Hardy of the *Mutine* spoke to a neutral ship which told him that the French had indeed taken Malta, but the main body of the fleet had sailed from there three days ago. Nelson quickly calculated that the enemy could only be heading for Egypt, where they could open up an alternative route to the British possessions in India. He called some of his favourite captains on board and asked them loaded questions to confirm his decision. Meanwhile, Captain Thompson of the *Leander* investigated two strange frigates on the horizon and found they were French. He signalled this to Nelson, but to his amazement he was told to rejoin the fleet. Nelson assumed that they were stragglers some way behind Bonaparte's fleet, but in fact they were outlying patrols. Further investigation

This was the moment Nelson had been waiting for, certainly since Hotham had failed to press the attack home in 1795; probably since his first entry to the navy; possibly since, as a child, he heard of the great victories of the Seven Years' War.

would have led to a great battle in which Bonaparte would probably have been taken, and the expedition stopped. In fact the French had left Malta rather later than Nelson believed, though they were indeed on their way to Egypt.

Despite the legend of the Band of Brothers, created by Nelson retrospectively to describe his officers in this campaign, he was in fact very lonely during the campaign of 1798. His staff aboard the flagship was young and inexperienced, and he had little contact with the captains of the other ships, except by signals or when they visited him in ones or twos when the winds were light. He had almost no news from home, and no frigates to scout for him. He was determined to keep his ships of the line close together, for he feared that the French might escape if he encountered them when they dispersed. Even his contact with home was unsatisfactory – 'You must be content with short letters', he told his wife. He bore a responsibility which is almost inconceivable in the modern world, with no-one to confirm or contradict his decisions.

The fleet made good speed by the most direct route to Alexandria, while Bonaparte clung to the coast of Crete on the way. As a result, Nelson got there first, and found the Egyptians amazed by his speculation. In an anxious frame of mind, he set sail almost immediately, which was unfortunate; Bonaparte's force arrived the next day and landed its men to take the city and go on to Cairo. Meanwhile Nelson headed north towards Turkey, then along the coast of Crete in unfavourable winds. He came to rest at Syracuse in Sicily. He wrote to Hamilton, 'I cannot find, or at this moment learn, beyond vague conjecture where the French fleet are gone to.' Rest and refreshment did something to ease his mind. As the fleet sailed after four days, he wrote, 'Surely watering at the fountain of Arethusa, we must have victory'.

At last, on 28 July off the coast of Greece, he found what he needed to

A map of the Nile Campaign illustrating the area east of Sicily with four tracks marked. The lowest and straightest one is Nelson's first passage to Alexandria in pursuit of the French. The next one up is Bonaparte's route, close to the coast of Crete. The zig-zag course is Nelson's voyage back to Sicily, mostly against the wind, and the route via southern Greece is Nelson's final passage to Alexandria to find and defeat the French. From Cooper Willyams, *A Voyage up the Mediterranean*. *The British Library 747 g20*

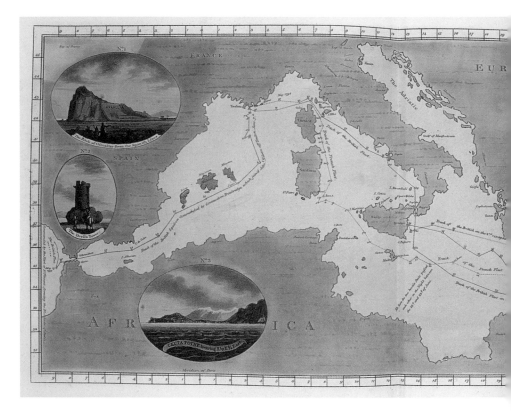

know. The Turkish governor had been informed of the invasion of Egypt, which was also a Turkish province. Again Nelson set sail for Alexandria, and made fast progress in a favourable wind. Early in the afternoon of 1 August he was off the city. His lookouts saw that the harbour was full of ships, and the French flag was flying everywhere. But where was the main fleet? As first there was despair that it might have been missed, and Captain Saumarez records that 'despondency nearly

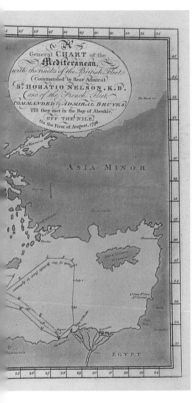

took possession of my mind, and I do not recollect ever to have felt so utterly hopeless or out of spirits ...' Around 2.30 the masthead lookouts in the *Zealous* and *Goliath* spotted the fleet at anchor in Aboukir Bay a few miles away. Lieutenant Wilkes of the *Goliath* perceived 'thirteen sail of the line, four large frigates and eight or ten corvettes, all moored in a most masterly state of defence with the *Orient* of 130 guns [actually 120] in the centre, apparently expecting our approach, situated as they were in a bay unknown to us, and at anchor infinitely superior.'

This was the moment Nelson had been waiting for, certainly since Hotham had failed to press the attack home in 1795; probably since his first entry to the navy; possibly since, as a child, he heard of the great victories of the Seven Years' War. He was a resolute, skilled commander with a well-drilled fleet, facing an enemy who had no escape route. Conventional wisdom would have suggested waiting for daylight, as night attacks were considered dangerous. Nelson never countenanced that, and ordered his ships to form up as most convenient. As it happened the *Goliath* under Captain Foley took the lead. As he approached the head of the enemy line, he spotted a key weakness in the enemy position. They were anchored too far from the shore, and there was room for him to pass ahead of the leading ship and attack it on the unprepared side, with devastating effect.

Four more ships followed Foley, each pounding the leading French ship then anchoring opposite an opponent in the line. In fact the French were far less prepared than they should have been. The leading ships of their line were old, weak and undermanned. Large parties had been sent ashore for water and firewood. The port guns of each ship, where Foley and the others were now attacking, were unmanned and unready. Though the French were stubborn, the first two ships of the line were soon beaten and their masts began to fall.

Nelson's *Vanguard* was the sixth ship of the impromptu British line. His contempt for the French had been growing over the years. Three months at St Omer had done nothing to rectify this, and on his return he had written, 'I hate their country and their manners'. He regarded the Revolution as a catastrophe for Europe. He witnessed its effects on the French navy at Toulon, and in constant reports of mutiny. 'I have just heard, that last night the crew of my neighbour [a French frigate] deposed their Captain, made the Lieutenant of Marines Captain of the Ship, the Sergeant of Marines Lieutenant of Marines, and their former Captain Sergeant of Marines. What a state! They are mad enough for any undertaking.' After his first brush with French ships in October 1793 he wrote, 'Had they been English, and we French, the case, I am sure, would have been very different.' Now he overheard the conversation of his men and was impressed with their calmness. 'I knew what stuff I had under me.' He could see that the shallow waters inshore of the French were becoming increasingly crowded with British ships. He directed the *Vanguard* towards the outside of their line, attacking the third ship, the *Spartiate*, which was also under attack from the other side but appeared undamaged.

At about 8.30, during the battle with the *Spartiate*, Nelson stood on the deck of the *Vanguard*, looking at a sketch of the bay which had been taken from a

Lord Nelson engaging the Toulon Fleet off the Mouth of the Nile.

French ship a few days earlier. A piece of langridge shot, made up of bolts and bars into a kind of cylinder, struck him on the forehead, making a wound three inches long which bared his cranium. He collapsed into Berry's arms, and the blood and the flap of skin obscured his left eye, blinding him. With typical morbidity he called out 'I am killed; remember me to my wife.' Down below in the cockpit, Surgeon Jefferson made light of the wound, though Nelson remained fatalistic. He tried to draft a final letter, but his wounded secretary was too overcome by emotion to continue, and it was dictated to his chaplain. However his injuries were not as serious as he had feared.

Nelson's own sketch of the Battle of
the Nile, showing the French fleet in
a straight line, with some detail of the
land and the British approaching from
the top right.
The British Library, Additional MS 18676

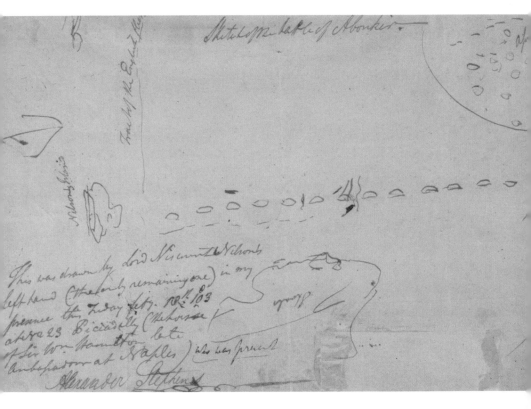

For several hours the battle went on without any direction from Nelson.
The British ships continued to deploy along the outside of the French line,
following the lead given by the *Vanguard*. Soon they came up against the mighty
120-gun *Orient* in the centre of the line, which had already seen off attacks by the
Majestic and *Bellerophon*. It was Ball in the *Alexander* who got the advantage on
her, firing his guns into her vulnerable quarter galleries while the *Swiftsure*

engaged her bows. A fire was started and got out of control. Nelson, beginning to recover, came on deck to see it. Before midnight (and times vary considerably in the ships' logs) the *Orient* exploded in a great cloud of flame, heard for miles around and terrifying all who saw it.

There was silence for some time after the great explosion, as officers and gun crews got over the shock. Only the *Majestic* and *Alexander*, conquerors of the *Orient*, carried the battle to what had been the rear of the enemy line. Around 4 a.m. Nelson returned to the deck to urge his ships on to action against the rest. He sent his flag lieutenant, Thomas Bladen Capel, round the least damaged ships and several more joined the action. Late in the morning Rear-Admiral Villeneuve, the senior surviving French officer, decided to escape with two undamaged ships of the line and two frigates. Nelson perhaps remembered what he had written after his argument with Admiral Hotham three years previously 'had we taken ten sail, and allowed the 11th to escape when it had been possible to have got at her, I could never have called it well done'. He signalled one of his few ships with undamaged rigging, Captain Hood's *Zealous*, and ordered him to intercept; but it was hopeless and the four ships escaped.

Nelson, in perhaps the greatest sea victory of all time, took or destroyed eleven ships of the line out of thirteen, along with frigates and sloops. Bonaparte's army of 35,000 men was isolated in Egypt and his campaign seemed doomed. It was the following day before the last two French ships in Aboukir Bay, driven aground and isolated, finally surrendered, but by midday on 2 August the battle was over. The British had 218 sailors killed and 677 wounded; the French had more than 5,000 'taken, drowned, burnt and missing'. Nelson was wounded and exhausted, his men were battered and tired, his ships largely immobile after the loss of masts and rigging. But he was master of the Mediterranean.

7

Honours were heaped on Nelson.
The King of Naples made him Duke of
Bronte, while the Sultan of Turkey
gave him an amazing clockwork
decoration called a chelengk.

Naples and decline

Nelson's biggest task after his great victory was to put his severely damaged
fleet in order. He tried to inform St Vincent of his success and how much the
Mediterranean situation had changed after one night of battle, but even that
was difficult. With no frigates, he sent a message by the 50-gun *Leander*, but
she would be captured off the coast of Crete. Later some of his missing frigates
arrived and he was able to send the brig *Mutine* to Naples with news of the
battle. Otherwise, reports were transmitted by rumour carried mainly by local
craft or by French newspapers. It was two months before the British government
knew for sure the extent of the victory.

Nelson slowly recovered from the effects of his wound. He now knew that
it was not mortal and his sight was not in danger, though Surgeon Jefferson
continued to treat him for the rest of the month. He held a public thanksgiving
on board his ship on 2 August, and recommended that other captains did the
same, but there was little time for celebration. The fleet, though victorious, was
still highly vulnerable to counter attack. Dismasted ships were fitted with 'jury'
or improvised rig, the least damaged of the prizes were repaired, and those which
could not be repaired in the time available were burned. Troubridge's *Culloden*,
damaged by grounding on the way into battle, was saved when it might have
been more effective to write her off; but that would have meant admitting to
losing a ship, and it would have damaged the career of Troubridge, one of
Nelson's favourite captains.

The victorious ships and their prizes sailed in two groups. Saumarez left
with one on 14 August 1798, and Nelson remained to blockade Alexandria until
the 19th, when he started for Naples with some of the ships which would need
still more repair. Winds were light until 15 September, when a storm damaged
the *Vanguard* yet again. The fleet limped into Naples on the 22nd, to a euphoric

Naples Sep.br 8th 1798
4

My dear dear Sir

how shall I begin what
shall I say to you. tis impossible
I can write for since Last
monday I am delirious with
Joy & assure you I have a feaver
caused by agitation & pleasure.
Good God what a Victory never
never has their been any thing
half so glorious so compleat
I fainted when I heard the
Joyfull news & fell on my side
& am hurt but what of that
I shou'd feil it a Glory to die
in such a cause no I would
not like to die till I see

reception. Sir William and Lady Hamilton were rowed out to the *Vanguard* with King Ferdinand of Naples, and Emma collapsed into Nelson's arms, exclaiming 'Is it possible?' Ashore the populace went wild. Every time Nelson appeared in the street he was fêted. He stayed with the Hamiltons, and Emma nursed him back to health with asses' milk. He received a batch of letters from home and Lady Nelson's gossip from Roundwood seemed trivial. '… my dear Fanny, unless you can game, and talk scandal, that is lies, most probably your company will never be coveted by country town tabbies.' He hoped that rewards for the Nile would give the chance to choose a grander house.

Honours were heaped on Nelson. The King of Naples made him Duke of Bronte, while the Sultan of Turkey gave him an amazing clockwork decoration called a chelengk. But the news from home was disappointing; he was to be made Baron Nelson of the Nile and Burnham Thorpe, the lowest grade of the peerage, whereas Jervis had been made an earl, two grades higher, after the

Battle of St Vincent. There were sound technical reasons for this, as Nelson was not a commander-in-chief, but there were other slights. Troubridge's contribution was not recognised because his ship was grounded; an old rival, Sir Sidney Smith, was given command of the forces off Egypt independent of Nelson, and with diplomatic orders which enjoined 'all admirals, generals and officers' to give him every assistance. Lady Hamilton offered comfort. 'If I was King of England I would make you the most noble puissant Duke Nelson, Marquis Nile, Earl Alexandria, Viscount Pyramid, Baron Crocodile and Prince Victory, that posterity might have you in all forms.' Acquaintances noticed Nelson's wounded pride. 'Pray sir, have you ever heard of the Battle of the Nile?' he asked an English visitor, asserting that it was unique for three reasons, and bowing as he mentioned each: '… first, for its having been fought at night; secondly, for its having been fought at anchor; and thirdly been gained by an admiral with one arm'.

Meanwhile his ships were repairing and he was taking an interest in the strategic situation in the seas around Italy, and in Naples itself. It was a beautiful but violent kingdom, comprising most of the southern half of Italy and the whole of Sicily. King Ferdinand was only interested in hunting and his Queen, Maria Carolina, ruled the country, much influenced by the Hamiltons. Nelson soon joined this ruling elite, and found himself in a very different world from the loneliness and Spartan existence of the Nile campaign. In November he decided on an amphibious attack on Livorno to the north, and before setting off he persuaded the king to use his forces, '*La plus belle armée d'Europe*', against the French in Rome. Nelson was completely successful in taking Livorno, and the Neapolitans advanced to the north to take Rome. But the French quickly regrouped and Ferdinand had to retreat. It became a rout, and he was forced to abandon mainland Italy. The Neapolitan royal family was rowed out and crammed on board Nelson's ships, now back off Naples, on the dark night of 21 December. They sailed two days later and on Christmas Eve the *Vanguard* was hit by yet another storm. The King's youngest son died in the arms of Lady Hamilton, who was heroic in looking after the royal family until the ships arrived at Palermo in Sicily.

In February, a civil war developed in the Kingdom of Naples as the royalists began a counter-revolution against the republicans, so-called 'Jacobins', who ran what they called the 'Parthenopean Republic'. Nelson's ships blockaded the ports of southern Italy while the royal army advanced from the south. In the Bay of Naples, Captain Foote of the frigate *Seahorse* accepted the surrender of republicans in the forts around the city, and was prepared to allow them to go into exile in France. Nelson arrived and cancelled this in the name of the King of Naples. 'That as to rebels and traitors, no power on earth has a right to stand

His relationship with Lady Hamilton was becoming increasingly physical, and later he wrote, 'I did remember well the 12th February and also the months afterwards. I shall never be sorry for the consequences.'

between their Gracious King and them; they must instantly throw themselves on the clemency of their sovereign, for no other terms will be allowed them.' As a result, hundreds of them were publicly executed amid scenes of great savagery. Nelson was even more involved in the prosecution of Caracciolo, a Neapolitan admiral who had supported the rebels. He was tried in the wardroom of HMS *Foudroyant* and hung from her yardarm, after Nelson had refused requests for clemency. His body was dumped in the water but was insufficiently weighted and a few days later it floated to the surface alongside the *Foudroyant*, to the obvious horror of the King who was present at the time.

It was an unfortunate period in Nelson's career, brought on by the reaction to the stress of the Nile campaign and perhaps affected by his head wound. By this time his most celebrated indiscretion was already taking form. His relationship with Lady Hamilton was becoming increasingly physical, and later he wrote, 'I did remember well the 12th February and also the months afterwards. I shall never be sorry for the consequences.' It is not clear whether this refers to 1799 or 1800, but certainly there were more opportunities in the earlier year, when both were together in Palermo. Lady Hamilton was despised by many in the upper classes for her humble origins and her vulgar self-promotion. However, she provided Nelson with a mother figure as well as a lover, with adulation, amusement and drama as well as beauty. She symbolised life in Italy, where Nelson was idolised, a contrast to life at home, where his main impressions were of the domesticity of Lady Nelson, years of boredom at Burnham Thorpe or adjusting to life with one arm after Tenerife. Sir William Hamilton knew about the affair and accepted it, and the three formed a *ménage à trois*, living in the same house when Nelson was not at sea. It was a strange situation in that or any other age. Many of Nelson's closest friends,

Opposite: Lady Emma Hamilton painted
at Dresden in 1800, as she travelled
back to England with Nelson and her
husband. Nelson later had this portrait
hung in his cabin at sea.
National Maritime Museum, A4288

including St Vincent and Thomas Troubridge, strongly disapproved and advised
him against it.

Outside Naples and Sicily, Nelson's forces were helping the Maltese, who
had revolted on hearing the news of the Nile and were blockading the French in
the capital Valetta. Nelson, preoccupied with Naples, paid little attention and there
were times when it seemed that the Maltese might have to give up. There was a
far greater crisis in April 1799, when the main French fleet escaped from Brest
under Admiral Bruix and joined with the Spanish to enter the Mediterranean.
St Vincent was still nominally in command, though in poor health, and much of
the responsibility devolved on Admiral Lord Keith. Nelson resisted orders to send
his ships of the line to a concentration of the main fleet at Minorca, because he
was still deeply involved in the campaign around Naples, and had personally
promised the King his support. Bruix's fleet did no real damage, and Keith failed
to bring it to battle. Nelson was rebuked for his disobedience. Concentration of
force was a principle which Nelson himself had always supported, when the main
enemy battlefleet was active. But in the Naples situation he had, contrary to his
character, dispersed his forces in land warfare and small-scale blockades. There
were serious doubts in the fleet and the government about his judgement, at
least in his present frame of mind.

This almost certainly weighed against him at the Admiralty in June, when
St Vincent left due to ill health. Keith was away for a time and Nelson was in
temporary command. But Keith was confirmed in the appointment and returned
in November 1799, much to Nelson's chagrin. Early in the next year Sir William
Hamilton read in the press that he had been superseded as ambassador to Naples.
Nelson's health was declining, his headaches were recurring and he spent a large
amount of time in bed. He wrote, 'Greenwich Hospital seems a fit retreat to me,

after evidently being thought unfit to command in the Mediterranean.' In April he sailed with the Hamiltons to Malta to support his friend Ball in the siege of Valetta. He was present when the *Guillaume Tell*, the last survivor of the French fleet at the Nile, was captured. It was a fitting end to his command, providing a last link with his moment of glory. In June he resigned and began the long journey home.

He decided to travel with the Hamiltons. Keith had refused to let them go in the *Foudroyant*, a large and powerful 80-gun ship. Lady Hamilton was now pregnant with Nelson's child and remembered vividly the experiences of the voyage to Palermo with the Neapolitan royal family. It was decided to travel overland through Austria and Germany in a bizarre but strangely triumphant journey. In Vienna they met Haydn, who had composed the Nelson Mass after hearing the news of the Nile. Lady Hamilton impressed foreigners who were unaware of the implications of her manners and accent but she repelled the upper-class Englishmen she encountered, such as Hugh Elliot in Dresden. She was 'without exception the most coarse, ill-mannered, disagreeable woman I ever met with.' The party sailed from Hamburg and on 6 November 1800 it arrived at Great Yarmouth.

If Nelson ever had any doubts about his place in the heart of the common people, they were now dispelled. As soon as the citizens of Great Yarmouth heard of his arrival, they turned out in great numbers. They took the horses from the shafts of his carriage and dragged it through the streets to an inn. He was given the freedom of the city and there was a *feu de joie* in his honour. It was as exhilarating as his arrival at Naples two years earlier, but all the more touching because it was his own country, and indeed his native Norfolk. He travelled to London and was cheered by the populace of every town he passed through.

Yet his behaviour did nothing to endear him to the moral guardians and the upper classes. Emma Hamilton, in England for the first time since her marriage to Sir William, was snubbed by the court and was not well treated by the press. She was the 'chief curiosity' which Sir William had brought home from his archaeological study in Naples, but was too fond of her food and showed signs of an 'unfortunate personal extension'. The press did not know that she was carrying Nelson's child. The admiral met his wife and father at Nerot's Hotel in St James's Street, London. He was publicly fêted by the Admiralty and the Lord Mayor, but treated Frances with open contempt, while appearing regularly with the Hamiltons. Lady Nelson had always been faithful to her husband. She looked after his ailing father, supported her husband through many difficult moments, and had spent the last few years trying to build a home for the absent admiral at Roundwood. She was cast aside, and by the end of the year it was clear that they were going to live apart. Meanwhile, Nelson faced social ostracism from the 'upper ten thousand' who controlled high society. It was perfectly normal for a man of position to keep a mistress, but not to flaunt his relationship as Nelson did. If the memories of the events at Naples and the Bruix campaign had begun to override those of St Vincent and the Nile, and if his affair with Lady Hamilton had done any more to alienate him from influential opinion, then Nelson's career might have ended there. But on the first day of 1801 he was promoted to vice-admiral and appointed to the Channel Fleet under his old friend St Vincent, with further opportunities to distinguish himself.

'Not a moment should be lost in attacking the Enemy: they will every day and hour be stronger; we shall never be so good a match for them as at this moment.'

Copenhagen and the Channel

Nelson arrived in Plymouth on 17 January 1801. The whole fleet cheered when his flag was hoisted on the foremast of the *San Josef*, the very ship he had captured by boarding at St Vincent. He was pleased to have his old friend Hardy as flag captain, though the state of the ship was much less satisfactory. He had to move into Hardy's cabin while his own was painted and the dockyard workmen dragged their feet, not believing that Nelson really meant to go to sea at that time of year.

Already Nelson was getting word of possible operations elsewhere. In December 1800 Russia's 'mad Czar', Paul I formed the League of Armed Neutrality with Sweden, Denmark and Prussia. This threatened to deny Britain the use of the Baltic, her main source of naval stores such as timber, tar and hemp for making rope. A fleet was assembled to enter the Baltic and take on any fleets, especially the Russian, which might oppose it. Nelson was hardly on board the *San Josef* when he wrote to Spencer, the First Lord of the Admiralty, with his views on how to conduct the war. It was not long before he was allocated to the fleet for the Baltic, though his present ship was too deep in the hull to be suitable. In the middle of February he was transferred to the *St George*, a three-decker of 98 guns, a typical flagship for a junior admiral.

Nelson was still not to be given a fully independent command, for even St Vincent did not trust him as a commander-in-chief. In November 1800 he wrote, 'He cannot bear confinement to any object; he is a partisan; his ship is always in the most dreadful disorder, and [he] never can become an officer fit to be placed where I am.' He was to be under Admiral Sir Hyde Parker, another mediocre officer, more noted for his caution than his ability. Perhaps it was believed that his prudence would counterbalance Nelson's hot-headedness. Nor was Nelson to be sent on detachment, as he had been in the Nile campaign, for

14

Hognas

Wasoy · Walsahaven

Vik

Domsten

Kulla

Gunnarstorp

Palskop

Lappen

Karnan

THE SOUND

14

10

4

Gilberg Head
Gilleleve Chap
Nakke Head

Hesborg Hill

Boggehead

Hornbeck

Hammar Mill

12

2

10

Cronenberg

72

Helsingborg

Helfingoer
or Elfineur

Teilgaara

Disken

79

Ra

Hammelbeck

5

71

14

Tegelbruk

Sletten

9

Glomslof

Nivaae

Kungsgard

Sophienberg

8

14

12

Saby

Uranburg

11

Huen I.

Orje

Asmundstorp

Rong Sted

7

8

Pilhaken

Smistrup

6

10

18

Landscrona

Wabek

6

8

Graen

30

Paper Mill

5

SpringForbi

7

12

Dogstorp

Taarbeck

18

Barseback

Woods Head

8

Fishing
Huts

Lodkoping

Charlotten Lund

8

Pinhall

7

6

7

Borby

3 Crowns

6

4

COPENHAGEN

5

3

4

4

Round Tower
& Observatory

7

Salt
holm

10

Flaskekroe

N. Flint

Sjolle

4

Widovre

Taarnbye

6

3

Amag

Hollen
derbye

4

S. Flint

Trindelen

Malmo

Dragoe

Draco Point

5

3

Limhamn
Lernacku

Kogekroe

5

Hylje

Fosjo

Bunkeflod

6

Little Ground

7

2

4

Hokoping

6

KIOGE

7

Broad
Ground

Koground

ingskroe

BAY

7

6

9

10

Hollevik

G. Hammar

Chalk

7

Skanor

Scale of Miles
1 2 3 4 5 6

D E N M A R K

S W E D E N

Previous page: The approaches to
Copenhagen. Nelson's fleet came from
the south of Amager Island.
The British Library, The Naval Chronicle,
vol VIII

high-level diplomacy was involved, and the issue might be settled without firing a shot. Parker himself would be in direct command of the fleet for the Baltic with Nelson, in a sense, as his main striking force.

The original plan was to attack the Danish fleet before the ice melted in the Russian naval bases and allowed them to join their allies. But Hyde Parker, recently married to a young bride, was in no hurry. As the fleet moved round the south coast to Great Yarmouth Nelson wrote to St Vincent, 'Time, my dear Lord, is our best Ally, and I hope I shall not give her up, as all our Allies have given us up. Our friend here is a little nervous about dark nights and fields of ice, but we must brace up; these are not times for nervous systems.' The fleet which eventually sailed from Yarmouth on 12 March consisted of two 98-gun ships as flagships, eight 74s, five 64s, (including the *Agamemnon*) two small two-deckers of 50–54 guns, and a substantial number of frigates and smaller vessels which would be useful in the shallow and intricate waters of Denmark and the Baltic.

In contrast to the early years of the Mediterranean campaign, Nelson's private life followed him to sea. He carried on a passionate correspondence with Lady Hamilton, using the alias of 'Mr and Mrs Thompson' to evade censors and spies. He wrote to Emma, 'It is your sex that rewards us; it is your sex who cherish our memories; and you, my dear, honoured friend, are, believe me, the *first*, and best of your sex.' When Emma gave birth to a girl at the end of January, Nelson could hardly contain himself in his *alter ego*. 'I believe Mrs Thompson's friend will go mad with joy. He swears he will drink your health in a bumper. I cannot write, I am so agitated by this young man at my elbow. I believe he is foolish; he does nothing but rave about you and her.' Lady Hamilton's child was in theory a secret, even from Sir William, though it is difficult to believe that he did not know that the child was Nelson's. She took the young Horatia to be

Nelson's private life followed him to sea. He carried on a passionate correspondence with Lady Hamilton, using the alias of 'Mr and Mrs Thompson' to evade censors and spies.

brought up at her own expense by a Mrs Gibson who lived in Little Titchfield Street, London.

In mid-March there was a political crisis when William Pitt, Prime Minister since 1783, resigned because the King would not support his plans for Roman Catholic Emancipation. The new government was headed by Henry Addington and was inclined towards peace. St Vincent rose to the top office in the navy as First Lord of the Admiralty. On the 23rd there was a political event of even greater consequence for Parker's expedition, though it was not known in the west for some weeks. Czar Paul I, prime mover of the League, was assassinated.

Off the Danish coast, Parker was undecided about whether to enter the Baltic through the Sound for a direct attack on Copenhagen or pass through the Great Belt, which would give him the chance to by-pass the city and head straight for the Russian Fleet (regarded by Nelson as the main object of the campaign) or to head north again to attack Copenhagen. His critics believed he was delaying the action. Nelson, still impatient, wrote to his chief, that 'not a moment should be lost in attacking the Enemy: they will every day and hour be stronger; we shall never be so good a match for them as at this moment.' Nelson persuaded him to go through the Sound, and on 30 March the fleet sailed in a single line past Kronenberg Castle, which opened up a heavy but ineffective fire.

The Danes relied on natural features and land fortresses, as well as the ships of their fleet, to defend themselves. Off Copenhagen the Middle Ground shoal restricted entry to the city to a narrow channel, which could be approached from the north or the south. Between the city and the shoal, the north end of the King's Channel was protected by an imposing citadel, though it was too far away to dominate the channel. The Three Crowns Battery had been built on piles out in the mud flats, with a smaller battery nearby. Down the rest of the Channel the

Previous pages: The Battle of
Copenhagen. The British fleet is placed
diagonally across the centre of the
picture, with the Danish ships and forts
behind it, and the city beyond that. To
the bottom left, bomb vessels fire over
the British fleet into the town.
National Maritime Museum, BHC0529

Danes anchored a force of ships of the line and static blockships to deter an
attack. But they were placed along the length of the channel, rather than across
it to block its ends. An approach into the King's Channel would certainly be
difficult, but it was not impossible.

Since the Three Crowns Battery was clearly the strongpoint of the defence,
it was decided to attack from the other end, the south. Nelson had already shifted
his flag from the *St George* to the *Elephant*, a 74 of familiar layout and commanded
by Thomas Foley of Nile fame. Nelson would lead the attack, while Parker
remained at anchor a little to the north with the reserve ships. On 1 April Nelson
took advantage of a northerly breeze to move his ships to the southern end of
the shoal, where they anchored. The Danes remained passive, and still did not
block the southern entrance. That night Nelson sent Captain Hardy out in a boat
to survey the waters, and he went more than a mile from the anchored British
ships, surveying right round the nearest Dane, whose sentries were less than alert.
Meanwhile Nelson had dinner with his immediate subordinate, Rear-Admiral
Thomas Graves. At 9.30 he began to consider the plan for the next day, with
Foley who had already proved his talent for inshore battle and Edward Riou
of the frigate *Amazon*, an outstanding captain who had impressed the admiral
when they first met the day before. The planning went on till 1 a.m., after which
Nelson's clerks wrote out copies of the orders for circulation to the ships.

As the sun rose next morning, the wind was from the south-south-east and
everything was ready for an attack. The pilots, mostly mates of merchant ships
from the Baltic trade, lost their nerve at first but were persuaded to go on.
Nelson's twelve ships of the line were to proceed up the enemy line, covering
Riou's force of frigates and sloops which would act as circumstances required.
Seven bomb vessels would anchor in shallow water between the ships of the line

and the Middle Ground and fire over the British fleet to the enemy ships and
the town itself.

There were difficulties to start with. The *Agamemnon* was unable to get
round the southern end of the shoal and never entered the action. The 74s *Bellona*
and *Russell* grounded further north, where they could still engage the enemy,
though not the fort which was their intended target. These ships marked the
way for the others, but the battle had not begun well, and the Danes opened a
devastating fire. For the first time in his career, Nelson faced the possibility of
defeat in a major battle. His life, of course, had been in danger many times.
During the Nile campaign there were several occasions when it seemed that he
had let an opportunity slip through his fingers, but once the enemy was found
the outcome was never in doubt. It was very different now though. The loss of
twelve ships of the line, and a great national humiliation, seemed likely. The glory
of the Nile would be cancelled out; Nelson, if still alive, would be in disgrace and
his reputation would be ambiguous, at best, to future historians.

Seeing his difficulties, Hyde Parker hoisted signal number 39, 'to break off
the action'. It is not clear whether he really intended it as a direct order, or
merely to cover Nelson from a charge of cowardice should he decide to retreat.
Nelson saw it and became agitated, rubbing the stump of his right arm, his 'fin',
as he did in such moments. He remarked to his flag captain, 'You know Foley,
I have only one eye – I have a right to be blind sometimes.' In his most famous,
if misunderstood gesture, he put his telescope to his blind eye and said 'I really do
not see the signal'. Riou and his frigates were now engaging the Three Crowns
Battery and were closer to Parker. Riou decided he had to obey, remarking 'What
will Nelson think of us?' He gave the order and was killed by a cannon ball
almost immediately.

Opposite: An illustration of the Danish
force drawn up outside Copenhagen,
showing ships, floating batteries
(with much less rigging) and the
Three Crowns Battery.
The British Library, Egerton MS 1614, f.50

The enemy fire began to slacken in the face of the powerful British
broadsides of guns. In some of the floating batteries, the officers appeared to have
lowered their flags in surrender, but the raw troops on board continued to fire.
Nelson drafted a letter to the Crown Prince, in charge of the Danish defences,
taking his time and affixing the grandest seal he had, as much to waste time as to
impress the Crown Prince. He addressed it 'To the Brothers of Englishmen, the
Danes' and went on: 'Lord Nelson has directions to spare Denmark, when no
longer resisting; but if the firing is continued on the part of Denmark, Lord Nelson
will be obliged to set on fire all the Floating-batteries he has taken, without having
the power of saving the brave Danes who have defended them.' It was a highly
ambiguous document, offering humanity but threatening the most painful of deaths
to those who resisted. It was reinforced by a letter to the government, stating 'Lord
Nelson's object in sending on shore a Flag of Truce is humanity.'

It has never become clear whether that was the real motive, or it was a *ruse
de guerre*. Though the British now had the upper hand, some of Nelson's ships,
including the *Elephant*, were still in difficulty and victory was far from certain.
In either case the Crown Prince accepted it at rather more than its face value
and agreed, after much negotiation, to a general truce for several weeks. In the
meantime the news of the death of the Czar arrived and the League of Armed
Neutrality collapsed, so further conflict was unnecessary.

The Battle of Copenhagen has entered the canon as one of Nelson's three
great victories. Yet it was far more ambiguous than the others. It was actually
settled by negotiation, and confirmed by changes in the diplomatic situation
which were well beyond Nelson's control. Danish naval officers created a myth
that they would have won had the Crown Prince not intervened, and that the
cease-fire was a stab in the back. For Nelson himself it had none of the triumph

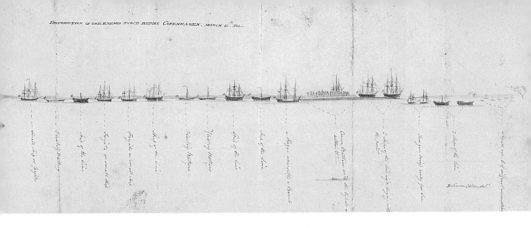

of the Nile, for he had no hatred for the Danes. Yet it was a great achievement, and it restored his career after a long dip. Parker was ordered home and Nelson became commander-in-chief.

Again, the victory was not acclaimed as much as it might have been by those in authority. Nelson was raised one rank in the peerage to Viscount, but still not to Earl to equal St Vincent. Parliament never gave a medal for Copenhagen, mainly because it might damage prospects of peace with Denmark. London never awarded him its highest honour, the freedom of the city, as it did to other victors of naval battles. Nelson was incensed that Hyde Parker figured too highly in what celebrations there were, though 'except being nearer the scene of the action, [he] had no more to do with that at Copenhagen than Lord St Vincent.'

Since the victory at the Nile the British had succeeded in building a great coalition against Bonaparte, including Turkey, Russia and Austria. The French defeated their land-based enemies one by one and by 1801 Britain was almost alone again against France. Nelson was back in England by the beginning of July that year and took command of a force to defend the country against invasion from a flotilla of barges in the French port of Boulogne. He hoisted his flag at Deal, in Kent, on 30 July, and jibbed at one of his duties – recruiting local fishermen and ferrymen for the Sea Fencibles, a kind of maritime home guard. 'The service, my dear Lord,' he wrote to St Vincent, 'above all others would be terrible for me: to get up and harangue like a Recruiting Serjeant! I do not think I could get through it; but as I am come forth, I feel that I might do this disagreeable service as well as any other.' He toured the area by frigate and demonstrated the seamanship which had stood him in good stead at the Nile and Copenhagen. In August 1801, with the help of the hydrographer Graeme Spence, he took the frigate *Medusa* through a channel south of Harwich, against the

Opposite: The French port of Boulogne,
showing the masts of invasion craft
massed in the small harbour.
The British Library, The Naval Chronicle,
vol XIV

advice of local pilots (the route bears the name Medusa Channel to this day). He
rallied the Sea Fencibles, but it was difficult to rely on them to turn out for drills.
'The men, I believe, will come forth, when the whole country prepares for
fighting; and all other business stands still; but they are no more willing to give
up their occupations than their superiors.'

Nelson worked out a detailed plan for the defence of the Thames estuary
involving blockships moored in the main channels and boats manned by Sea
Fencibles. As always he was more interested in a direct attack on the enemy, in
port if necessary, and he began to plan for an operation against Boulogne on the
French mainland. He was particularly interested in the French invasion craft
moored outside the harbour, which was too small and too tidal to contain a large
enough force. An attack on the craft by mortar vessels on the night of 3–4 August
did some damage. Nelson, now convinced that the harbour at Boulogne was not
suitable for a large invasion force turned his eyes to Flushing, which he regarded
as a more likely assembly point for the enemy. This was not approved by the
Admiralty, and on 15 August he assembled a force of five ships off Boulogne,
supported by fourteen flat boats armed with howitzers and carronades, and with
nearly sixty ships' boats to land seamen. They set off at 11.30 that night, planning
to destroy or cut loose the French barges. Nelson's boats became separated in the
dark night and unfamiliar currents and the French barges were harder to deal
with than expected, as most of them were aground at the time and could not
be sailed away. Worst of all, Nelson had underestimated the enemy fire from the
heights above the beaches. The invasion barges were 'filled with volleys upon
volleys of Musketry … It was impossible to remain on board, even to burn them.'
Forty-four men were killed and 128 wounded. Nelson was optimistic that the
enemy 'must have suffered equally with us', but it was certainly a defeat.

Boulogne

There was a recurring pattern in Nelson's career, in which glorious success was not sufficiently recognised, and was followed by failure. Perhaps it was coincidence, perhaps he had an inevitable tendency to over-reach himself. After his rapid advance in the American War, his command in the West Indies left him out of favour where it mattered. After St Vincent, came the disaster of Tenerife. After the Nile, a series of errors of judgement at Naples. And now, in the aftermath of Copenhagen, another misconceived amphibious operation. Compared with previous disasters, Boulogne had a minor effect on Nelson's career. He suffered no injury himself, and after two victories in fleet battles his reputation was strong enough to carry him through. One gentleman threatened to publish a scurrilous article on the expedition, unless he was paid £100. Nelson replied to the *poste restante* address he was given, but asked the Secretary of the Admiralty to station men to attempt to catch the blackmailer.

Early in October Nelson's orders for dealing with vessels suspected of being on the way to France were changed, and he immediately detected that something was afoot. 'What can this order from the Admiralty mean? Is it a sign of peace?' It was a fair question, for the Treaty of Amiens was signed that month between Britain and France, bringing more than eight years of war to an end in a rather unsatisfactory deal. On the 22nd he began a leave of absence.

The peace of Amiens

Nelson noticed some long faces among his officers at the prospect of peace, but he was ready for a rest. During the summer he and Lady Hamilton had decided to set up a home in the country, but within reach of London. They chose a house at Merton, to the south of the city, and ignored a survey which deplored 'a dirty, black-looking canal … which keeps the whole place damp.' Sir William, Emma and Horatio would keep their own residences in the city, but Sir William would be welcome at Merton at any time, and would pay a third of the costs. He was not allowed to bring his books and furnishings however, for Emma and Horatio wanted to set their stamp on the place. It was the first time Emma had decorated a home of her own and she filled it with portraits of herself and Nelson, and mementoes of his battles. Lord Minto, an old friend of Nelson's, found its inherent vanity 'such as to make me angry as well as melancholy'.

On 18 December Lady Nelson wrote to her husband. She offered to share 'a comfortable warm house' and begged him, 'Do, my dear husband, let us live together. I can never be happy until such an event takes place.' But whatever Nelson was looking for, it was not comfort. He returned the letter, marked 'opened in error'. It was her last and the break was now complete. His relations with his father were little better. During the 1790s Reverend Nelson had grown increasingly close to Lady Nelson at Burnham Thorpe, and wanted to maintain the link with his daughter-in-law. Frances thought it improper that they should live together in the circumstances and Nelson was opposed to the arrangement, which did not help relations between father and son. A reconciliation seemed possible in the spring of 1802, when Reverend Nelson planned to visit Merton, but the old man died at Bath on 27 April. Nelson had already arranged to attend a christening on the day of the funeral and it went ahead, though his household did wear black armbands.

Previous page; A bust of Nelson
in 1801, aged forty-three,
by John Flaxman.
National Maritime Museum, 2549

At Merton, Nelson had his first period of real rest for eight years, apart from the time in 1797–98 when he was recovering from his wounds. The *ménage à trois* was a strange affair by any standards, though outwardly its participants gloried in it, and called themselves the *Trio Juncta in Uno* – three joined in one. Sir William was presumably happy with the classical associations of the phrase, while for Nelson it had religious significance as representing the Holy Trinity, and perhaps a naval resonance – rope, the essence of naval seamanship, was made up of three strands joined into one, a ship had three masts, a large one had three decks and a fleet had three squadrons. Nelson worshipped Lady Hamilton, in a way which seemed inexplicable to many of his friends. He planned to have his daughter Horatia as a permanent resident, but Emma continually delayed this while her husband was alive, and the child's visits were infrequent. Nelson was not pleased with the constant snubs from high society, or the paucity of important visitors; but his eighteen months of peace at Merton were as close to real happiness as he ever came. He referred to it as 'Paradise Merton'.

The exact nature of the relationship between Nelson and Emma Hamilton is still something of a mystery. It has never been clear exactly when it began in the fullest sense. It was obviously passionate enough on an emotional level, though it only produced one child, and neither partner was infertile; contraception was highly unlikely in the circumstances, and this might suggest that it involved less physical passion than one might expect. Lady Hamilton was large and loving, and clearly fulfilled Nelson's long-standing need for a mother figure. She was a courageous and resourceful woman and just as patriotic as Nelson. He saw her as a suitable companion for a great hero, in contrast to the quiet and staid Lady Nelson. He was blind to Emma's faults, though Nelson's fellow officers saw her as vulgar and lacking in taste and decorum.

A bust of Nelson's daughter Horatia at the age of ten, by Christopher Prosperi.
National Maritime Museum, D7573

Sir William was old enough to be a father figure, but the relationship was far more complex. Besides his own father, Nelson had always found captains and admirals, such as Maurice Suckling and St Vincent, to fill that role. It is ironic that the affair with Lady Hamilton strained Nelson's relations with both St Vincent and his real father. Nelson had a great respect for Hamilton, almost amounting to love, and this was reciprocated by Sir William, who was pleased to have the company of the great admiral. Sir William was seventy-one in 1801, a considerable age at the time. He had perhaps lost any physical attractiveness he might have had for Emma, and possibly his taste for sexual activity, but she too continued to regard him as a father figure.

Nelson was quick to take up his place in the House of Lords as Viscount Nelson. He made his maiden speech on 29 October 1801, supporting a motion that Sir James Saumarez, his second-in-command at the Nile, should be given the thanks of the house for an action with the French near Gibraltar. He

The house at Merton, south of London,
drawn by Thomas Baxter. The bridge
spans an artificial canal called 'the Nile'.
National Maritime Museum, 8252-A

generously asserted that 'a greater action was never fought', praised Lords Hood
and St Vincent who had trained both Saumarez and Nelson in fleet tactics,
and sat down to cries of 'hear, hear!' It was, he wrote modestly, 'bad enough,
but well meant'.

Nelson was technically on leave for six months until 10 April 1802, when
to his amusement he received orders to 'strike my flag *and come on shore*' – though
actually he had been on shore for some time. Though he was on half pay

he continued to take an interest in the development of his profession, and
particularly on the two long-term constraints on British naval power – timber
and seamen.

His paper on seamen, produced in February 1803, was not unsympathetic
to the problems of the lower deck, though it showed a certain naivety – 'Their
pay and provisions cannot possibly be improved from what they are at present'.
He was much concerned with desertion, and he believed that as many as 42,000

men had run from the navy in the last war. He suggested that each man should receive a certificate after five years service, having 'never been concerned in mutinies, nor deserted', and would receive two guineas (£2.10) 'every New Year's Day, or on the King's birth-day' for the rest of his life. After eight years this would go up to four guineas. It was quite far-sighted, and anticipated the system of good-conduct pay and pensions which became standard in the mid-Victorian navy, but for the moment it was beyond the political will of the nation. Nelson recognised that it would cost 'an enormous sum', and it remained just one of many pamphlets and proposals to improve naval recruitment and to ease the brutality of the press gang.

In July both Nelson and Sir William received honorary degrees from Oxford University, and the three decided to make a tour into Wales, where Sir William had estates. It was Nelson's only excursion in the British Isles, outside his normal range of Norfolk, London, Bath and the naval ports. On the way Nelson received the freedom of the towns of Monmouth, Hereford and Worcester, where he gave due credit for his naval success. 'It was my good fortune to have under my command some of the most experienced Officers in the English Navy, whose professional skill was seconded by the undaunted courage of British sailors; and whatever merit might attach itself to me, I must declare, that I had only to show them the Enemy, and Victory crowned the standard.' He examined the Forest of Dean, 'about 23,000 acres of the finest land in the Kingdom', and suggested ways in which its timber might be better managed to meet the insatiable demands of the navy.

Nelson remained bitter about the lack of recognition for Copenhagen, and lobbied constantly to get his former subordinates rewarded. He was short of money and petitioned the Prime Minister unsuccessfully for an increase in

'It was my good fortune to have under my command some of the most experienced Officers in the English Navy, whose professional skill was seconded by the undaunted courage of British sailors; and whatever merit might attach itself to me, I must declare, that I had only to show them the Enemy, and Victory crowned the standard.'

pension. In November 1802 he seconded the Address in the House of Lords for the first Parliament since the Union with Ireland. In December he spoke in the House again, on a subject which had troubled him since his days in Antigua fifteen years earlier – naval corruption. St Vincent had proposed a bill to set up a Commission of Enquiry into abuses of the system and Nelson spoke in his absence. He gave general support, but was unhappy about clauses which gave the commission power to look into the papers of individual merchants dealing with the navy. '… the credit of the British Merchant is the support of the commerce of the world; his books are not lightly, nor for any ordinary purpose, to be taken out of his own hands; the secrets of his business are not to be too curiously pried into.' In February 1803 he had the unpleasant task of appearing as a character witness at the trial of Colonel Despard, who had served with him in the Nicaragua expedition more than twenty years before. He testified that he was 'a brave officer and honourable and loyal man', but the judge dismissed this and sentenced Despard and his fellow accused to be hanged, drawn and quartered for treason; later the King remitted this to simple hanging and beheading. In April Nelson gave evidence before the Commission of Naval Enquiry into alleged corruption, and highlighted the delays in paying prize money to the seamen, and the difficulties if a Prize Agent went bankrupt.

In March 1803, as relations with France worsened once again, the British government launched what might be called a pre-emptive strike – not against the enemy, but against its own seamen. In great secrecy, press warrants were issued to the officers in the main naval ports, and press gangs backed up by marines set out through the towns and harbours, taking men into the navy before they had any inkling that anything was afoot. The 'hot press' of 1803 had begun, and there could be little doubt that war, if it came, would soon involve Britain's great naval hero.

'War or Peace? Every person has a
different opinion. I fear perhaps the
former, as I hope so much the latter.'

10

Commander-in-Chief, Mediterranean

In March 1803 Nelson still did not know his immediate future. 'War or Peace? Every person has a different opinion. I fear perhaps the former, as I hope so much the latter.' He already knew that in the event of war he would be recalled to service as commander-in-chief of the Mediterranean Fleet, and that his flagship would be the 100-gun *Victory*. Thus began an association of names of great historic resonance. But there would be several near-separations before the two were finally and indelibly joined.

The *Victory* was already more than forty years old, and Nelson knew her well as Jervis's flagship at St Vincent. After that she had been reduced to a hospital ship for prisoners in the River Medway. She was rescued and given a 'great repair' in Chatham Dockyard. It cost over £70,000, more than the cost of the original ship in 1765, showing that St Vincent was prepared to go to some length to preserve her. Superficially she was much changed, but her fine sailing qualities remained intact.

Nelson was distracted when his great friend Sir William Hamilton became gravely ill and died on 6 April. He had lost a learned mentor, and perhaps even a father figure. 'Poor Lady Hamilton', he wrote, was desolate. 'I hope she will be left properly; but I doubt.' He took a good deal of interest in the appointment of officers to the *Victory*, and had enough influence at the Admiralty to get his way. He sent a list of six lieutenants, out of a complement of eight, 'which will be enough to begin with'. By 17 April, when the youngest son of a distinguished admiral applied for a post as lieutenant, he was too late. Nelson told the Duke of Clarence 'I agree with your Royal Highness most entirely, that the son of

a Rodney ought to be the protégé of every person in the Kingdom, and particularly of the Sea-Officers [but] she is full, and I have twenty on my list.'

The senior Lieutenant was John Quillam, a Manxman from the Isle of Man, who had been born in 1771 and had come into the navy the hard way. His chaplain and diplomatic secretary, Alexander John Scott, had 'abilities of a very superior cast' and Surgeon George Magrath was, according to Nelson, 'by far the most able medical man I have ever seen'. Nelson's opinion of Thomas Atkinson, who had served under him at Tenerife and Copenhagen, was still high – 'the best Master I ever knew'.

But Nelson was still not secure in his possession of his own flagship. The Mediterranean Fleet had to take third place to the North Sea Fleet and the Channel Fleet, which would directly protect Britain against invasion from France. When it was casually suggested that the *Victory* might be needed in the North Sea, Nelson was alarmed and pointed out that 'all my things, servants, wines etc, etc, are ordered to be sent to her, be where she will – even my sheep, poultry, hay, corn and every comfort are ordered to her'.

The ship was sailed round to Portsmouth after fitting out at Chatham and Nelson arrived there early in the afternoon of the 18th May, the same day as war was declared with France.

The war was a strange one. The British government had reacted to its fears about the ambition of Napoleon, rather than any concrete threat. With no allies they had no real way of striking back at the French, except to restrict their trade and the movements of their fleets. The French, in turn, began to prepare for an invasion of southern England, despite the weakness of their sea power.

Nelson's role in all this was mainly to control the rebuilt French Toulon fleet, which might escape into the Atlantic and intervene in the English Channel.

Victory off Toulon Octr. 21: 1803

My Dear Child

 receive this first Letter
from your most affectionate Father
If I live it will be my pride to see
you Virtuously brought up, but
if it pleases God to call me I trust
to himself, in that case, I have left
Dear Lady Hamilton your Guardian
I therefore charge you my child on
the value of a Fathers Blessing to
be Obedient and attentive to all
her kind admonitions and instruct:
ons, at this moment I have left you
a codicil dated the sixth of September

He was rowed out to the *Victory* and at 3.30 in the afternoon of the 18th his flag was hoisted at the foremast. The next day he wrote to St Vincent 'If the Devil stands at the door, the Victory shall sail tomorrow forenoon.' But a crew might mutiny if sent on foreign service without being paid. The payment began at eight in the morning and took several hours. It was early in the afternoon of Saturday the 20th when she sailed, in company with the frigate *Amphion*.

Still Nelson was not at ease. His orders were to find Admiral Cornwallis with the Channel Fleet of Brest, and then turn the *Victory* over to him if he needed her to reinforce his own command. He was off Brest two days later, but there was no sign of the fleet. Nelson stayed there for more than a day, 'not in a little fret'. He transferred his most urgent personal goods to the *Amphion*, sailing for the Mediterranean at 6.30 in the evening of the 23rd and leaving a message for Cornwallis. 'If you have no commands for the *Victory* I trust you will order her to join me without a moment's notice.' It was an unfortunate choice, for Cornwallis arrived at noon on the 25th. Indeed he did not need the *Victory* and sent her on with all dispatch; but of course she sailed much slower than the *Amphion*, and for the next two months Nelson had to live in the cramped quarters of a frigate, rather than the *Victory's* great cabin. In the *Amphion* he arrived off Toulon on 8 July, and the *Victory* did not arrive until three weeks later.

In many ways the Mediterranean command was the best in the Royal Navy – the largest, and closest to home, of the overseas fleets. In the home fleets, in the Channel and North Sea, or the ports commands at Plymouth, Portsmouth and the Nore, the admiral was always under the eye of the Admiralty. The home commander did not have the right to promote his subordinates; the Commander-in-Chief of the Mediterranean Fleet could advance officers up to the rank of captain to fill vacancies. Prize money was also very attractive on the

Nelson's cabin on board the *Victory* as it is today. On the table are quill pens and writing paper. It is obviously quite comfortable by naval standards, but all this would have to be cleared away when the ship went into battle.
Portsmouth Historic Dockyard

Mediterranean Station, with *carte blanche* to raid French commerce throughout a sea which the enemy regarded as his own. The other main overseas commands, in the East and West Indies, were even freer from Admiralty interference, and the West Indies also offered excellent opportunities for prize money, but the fleets on these stations were much smaller, and were not expected to face the might of the enemy battle fleet.

The geographical title of the fleet was not to be taken too literally. In the past it generally meant the western Mediterranean, until Bonaparte's expedition to Egypt, and Nelson's response, had opened eyes to the possibilities east of Italy. It was not confined to the sea itself, but traditionally included the Gibraltar base at the entrance, and the Spanish base at Cadiz some fifty miles outside. Within two-and-a-half years Nelson was to show just how liberally the term Mediterranean Fleet could be interpreted. It had three main aims; to destroy enemy trade in the area, to support Britain's allies and potential allies and to neutralise the French fleet at Toulon. It was not the first time Nelson had taken on enormous responsibilities, and he never shrank from them; but it was to be a far more drawn-out affair than the Nile campaign demanding high levels of organisation, diplomacy and above all patience. Now aged forty-four, Nelson had matured enough to add these qualities to his well-established ones of charisma, daring, seamanship and tactical skill.

In contrast to his first period in the Mediterranean Fleet, from 1793–97, Nelson saw little action. Commanders-in-chief were not expected to get involved in fighting expect in a general fleet battle, and the *Victory* was far too clumsy and expensive to chase privateers or engage frigates. Furthermore, the British had no allies in the area, and there was no aggressive policy from the government, so no need for amphibious landings or evacuations.

Already the victor of two unprecedented fleet battles, Nelson had far less to prove than in the past. He was constantly hopeful that the war would not last long, that the French would tire of it or a great fleet battle would settle the issue. But this was not to be, and became even less likely when William Pitt, who had opposed the peace of 1801, returned to power in May 1804. In compensation, however, Nelson had a strong and congenial staff on board his flagship, and many friends in the ships and in diplomatic posts around the Mediterranean.

Dr Leonard Gillespie, the new Physician of the Fleet, arrived on board on 2 January 1805. He painted a very rosy picture of life on board the flagship, and admired Nelson. His 'noble frankness of manner, freedom from vain personal formality and pomp (so necessary to the decoration of empty little men), can only be equalled by the unexampled glory of his naval career and the watchful and persevering diligence with which he commands the fleet.' Gillespie found that his duties were light, because health was so good. Only one man out of 840 in the ship was sick and the other ships of the fleet, also part of Gillespie's practice, were in equally good condition. Nelson and his officers do not appear to have been overworked either, at least in good weather.

Gillespie was wakened by his servant at six every morning and had breakfast in the admiral's cabin with 'Lord Nelson, Rear-Admiral Murray, the Captain of the Fleet, Captain Hardy, Commander of the *Victory*, the Chaplain, the secretary, one or two officers of the ship'. Business was carried out between the hours of seven and two, and at 2.45 the tune 'The Roast Beef of Old England' announced the Admiral's dinner, generally consisting of 'three courses and a dessert of the choicest fruit, together with three or four of the best wines, champagne and claret not excepted; and what exceeds the relish of the best viands and most exquisite wines, if a person does not feel himself perfectly at ease it must be his own fault, such is the urbanity and hospitality which reign here, notwithstanding the four orders of Knighthood worn by Lord Nelson and the well-earned laurels which he has acquired.' Bands played, officers walked the deck, and Gillespie suggests an atmosphere not unlike a good hotel. There was tea at six, and more conversation with his lordship 'who at this time generally unbends himself, though he is at all times as free from stiffness and pomp as a regard to proper dignity will admit, and is very communicative.' Punch and cakes were served at eight, and those who favoured an early night were in bed an hour later.

St Vincent's extremely close blockade of Cadiz was like a cork in a bottle. Nelson's more distant blockade of Toulon was more like a cat waiting outside a mousehole. In his heart Nelson wanted a brief and decisive fleet battle, not the long-term, but wearing and expensive, strategic advantage which might be gained by blockade. He wrote of his 'intention to try every possible means to induce the French Fleet at Toulon to put to sea.' As part of that strategy, the blockade must not be too tight. The main fleet was out of sight of the port, with frigates watching it. Captain Whitby, who commanded the *Belleisle* for a short time in the fleet, was critical of Nelson's system. 'First, then, he does not cruise upon his rendezvous; second, I have consequently repeatedly known him from a week to three weeks, and even a month, unfound by ships sent to reconnoitre … thirdly, he is occasionally obliged to take the whole squadron in to water, a great distance from Toulon.'

Nelson's main problem was the lack of suitable bases, particularly since he had decided to keep his fleet together and take all his ships away to water at once. Minorca was ideally situated but had been given back to the Spanish. Gibraltar, 700 miles away, had no protected harbour and no supplies of its own. Malta had better harbours, but few supplies and was a three-week voyage away. Nelson wrote, 'The fleet can never go there if I can find any other corner to put them in.' Instead he began to develop a new anchorage among the Maddelena Islands, at the northern end of neutral Sardinia. The area had been surveyed by Captain Ryves of HMS *Agincourt* at the end of the last war, and Nelson used his chart to anchor there at the end of October. 'After various tacks, and being close to the two rocks in Captain Ryves's chart, and abreast the rocks where he was, the whole squadron anchored at six o'clock in the evening, without any accident, in Agincourt Sound, under the Sardinian shore.' Nelson had to do much negotiation to keep the anchorage open, but he regarded it as 'one of the finest harbours I have ever seen'.

One of Nelson's most onerous responsibilities was to keep his fleet supplied with the necessities of life, and he could not always rely on support from home. The first requisite for good health at sea was diet, and that largely depended, in the days before refrigeration and tinned food, on regular supplies of fresh food. Naval food has always been a subject of propaganda and jokes – pamphleteers

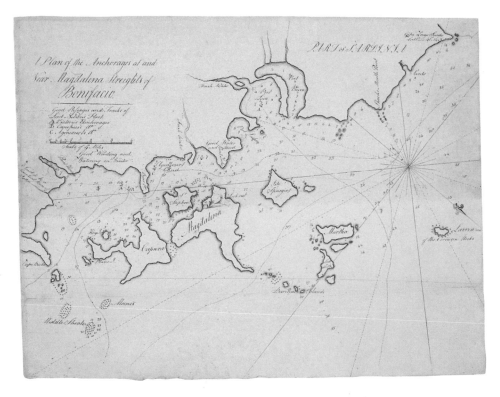

wrote of trouser buttons carved out of meat, or biscuit infested with insects.
The writers of these articles knew very little about how much the admirals cared
about feeding their men, how proud they were when their crews were healthy.
In May 1804 Nelson was of the opinion that 'the health of this Fleet cannot be
exceeded.' Scurvy was under control, but not completely eliminated, and old
cases might recur. In May 1804 Nelson found that thirty-seven men of one of his

ships were inflicted with 'an inveterate scurvy' and the Physician of the Fleet informed him that they needed 'six ounces of lemon juice, and two ounces of sugar, daily, in addition to the present quantity issued by the Purser, for the space of twelve days'.

Much of the meat supply came from North Africa and Nelson had to keep good relations with the rulers there, despite cultural and religious differences and their habit of raiding European commerce. He wrote from the *Victory* in May 1804, 'our government wish to avoid, if possible, a quarrel with the Dey [of Algiers]'. Early in June he was concerned with a British privateer which had offended the Bey of Tunis, and almost caused a rift. He lamented that 'Naval Commanders have no authority whatever over these Pirates.' He also took a good deal of interest in the men's clothing. In June 1804 he ordered the naval agent in Malta to purchase cotton there, enough to make 5,000 banyans (loose shirts), and pairs of trousers.

Nelson had to spread his ships beyond the area of Toulon itself. On a typical day, 21 June 1804, the main fleet was off Toulon as usual with eight of the line and seven smaller vessels under Nelson's direct control. Two frigates were just outside the Straits of Gibraltar, 'for the protection of our Trade bound into the Mediterranean, and the destruction of the Enemy's Privateers and Cruisers.' Two more were just inside the Straits with similar aims, and to help the garrison of Gibraltar when needed. Five ships were patrolling to keep the Adriatic open to trade and prevent an attack on Greece. The frigate *Juno* was off Barcelona to pick up intelligence about a Spanish declaration of war. Other ships were in transit to Malta or Gibraltar for minor repairs, or to rendezvous with supply ships. There was no sign of the French coming out and in August Nelson wrote that 'we have a uniform sameness, day after day, and month after month – gales of wind for ever'. In September 1804 he complained that he had not set foot outside his ship for fifteen months. By November he was complaining of 'frequent pains in his right side, from former injuries – that many warnings and inabilities made him conscious of his shattered frame, and anxious for repose.'

At last, in January 1805, the French made their first move. Nelson's fleet was taking on water in the Maddelenas on the 19th when two frigates arrived with the news that the enemy had sailed from Toulon the day before, with two other British frigates in pursuit. Nelson instantly ordered his ships to sea, and he was not to know that the French would quickly turn back after storm damage. He last heard of them heading south from Toulon and the wind patterns suggested that they must go east. On checking that the phantom fleet had not been seen in any of the likely areas of Naples, Sardinia or Sicily, he repeated his exploits of 1798, and headed for Alexandria, arriving on 8 February. He found 'three Turkish frigates, not more than 300 bad soldiers, and in short, not the least probability of making a defence had they been so inclined' – but no sign of the French. On the way back westward he explained himself to the First Lord of the Admiralty. 'Feeling, as I do, that I am entirely responsible for the whole of my conduct, I find no difficulty at the moment, when I am so unhappy at not finding the French, nor having obtained the smallest information where they are, to lay before you the whole of the reasons which induced me to pursue the line of conduct I have done.'

The French continued to use Nelson's absences from the station to attempt escape. On April 4, when he was anchored off Sardinia, the frigate *Phoebe* arrived at 10 a.m. with the news that the French were heading south from Toulon. This time, though Nelson did not know it yet, he was about to take part in the greatest maritime chase in history.

11

The Trafalgar Campaign

Nelson had no way of knowing if this French breakout was any more threatening than the last, but in fact it was part of the Emperor Napoleon's grand plan to defeat the British. Little had changed in two years of war. The British still had no major allies on land, the French still threatened invasion of England. But the Emperor was beginning to realise that his original plan, to frighten the British or invade them by stealth, was not going to work. The British were much more united and determined than he had imagined, and his idea of getting the invasion barges across the English Channel in darkness and calm weather was clearly not going to work in the face of British naval superiority. Instead he relied on subterfuge to get French naval superiority in the area. Nelson was to be lured to the West Indies and the Toulon fleet, under Admiral Villeneuve, would then slip back across the Atlantic to join the Spanish and the rest of the French fleet, to clear the Channel and prepare the way for an invasion of England.

Nelson sent frigates to cover the possible routes for the enemy, and his first guess was that they would head for Naples and Sicily. But by 16 April 1805 he had received reports of them heading west towards the Straits of Gibraltar, and decided to follow them though he was some days behind. He stopped at Tetuan Bay, Morocco, for water and at Gibraltar for other provisions, and sailed on 6 May, a month after hearing the news. He had already guessed that they were headed for the West Indies, though he had to leave ships behind to cover other eventualities. He took a force of ten ships of the line and three frigates.

As the fleet followed the trade winds across the Atlantic, Nelson addressed the crew of the *Victory*. According to Gunner William Rivers he told them that he expected and hoped to fall in with the French fleet before they reached Barbados. 'I have it from good authority that they have 15 sail of the line and we have only 13. I am very sure every ship will easily manage one each when there

Previous page: Nelson's Trafalgar
uniform, showing the stars of his orders
and the bullet hole in its left shoulder.
National Maritime Museum, B 9701-B

will be two left for us, and it be very harsh indeed if we are not able to give a
very good account of them.' After this 'pretty and laconic speech' the men gave
him three cheers.

The fleet was at Barbados on 4 June, after a month's passage. Nelson had
gained rapidly on the enemy, who were now at Martinique, a hundred miles to
the north-west. Unfortunately he received a report that a large fleet had been
seen heading south, and he steered for Trinidad to try to intercept it; in fact the
report was mistaken and the French actually headed north to begin their voyage
home. As soon as he got more accurate intelligence Nelson set off in pursuit,
a few days behind. He now realised what was happening and sent the *Curieux*,
a fast-sailing brig captured from the French, with a message to the Admiralty.

This proved to be of great strategic importance. Lord Barham, the new First
Lord of the Admiralty, was able to re-position his fleets in time, and Villeneuve's
force was met by a British fleet under Sir Robert Calder off Cape Finisterre.
There was an indecisive action in fog and Villeneuve retreated into the northern
Spanish ports of Vigo and Corunna.

Meanwhile Nelson's fleet crossed the Atlantic again and anchored at
Gibraltar on 20 July. He went ashore, leaving the decks of the *Victory* for the
first time in nearly two years, since he had transferred to her from the frigate
Amphion. After replenishing his ships he sailed north, still in search of the enemy,
and on 15 August he met the Channel Fleet off Gibraltar, where he was informed
of recent events on that side of the Atlantic. Its commander-in-chief, Cornwallis,
had orders to take most of Nelson's ships under his command, but to send the
admiral himself home in HMS *Victory*. He arrived off Portsmouth on the 18th,
to strike his flag and make his way to Merton.

His daughter Horatia was already there, and there was a steady stream of visitors from Nelson's past, including the Duke of Clarence, Lord Minto and Sir Peter Parker. According to the latter, 'I had a most hearty welcome. He looks remarkably well and full of spirits. His conversation is a cordial in these low times.' Nelson was there when Captain Thomas Blackwood arrived at five in the morning of 2 September on the way from the fleet to London, with urgent news. Villeneuve's fleet had gone to Cadiz, where it united with the Spanish to form a huge Combined Fleet of more than 30 ships of the line. A new British fleet would be needed to blockade or destroy it, and no-one had much doubt about who would lead it. There are two contradictory accounts of his reaction. One claims that he saw the opportunity immediately, saying 'Depend on it, Blackwood, I shall yet give Mr. Villeneuve a drubbing.' Another has him much more nonchalant. 'All this was nothing to him. "Let the man trudge it who has lost his budget"' was his obscure comment.

According to Lady Hamilton, she was stoical about losing her lover after such a short time. 'Even in this last fatal victory, it was I bid him go forth. Did he not pat me on the back, call me brave Emma, and said, "If there were more Emmas there would be more Nelsons."' In any case, Nelson set off for London to meet Lord Barham. A list of the fleet was placed in his hand and Barham told him to choose his own officers and ships. Nelson is said to have replied, 'Choose yourself, my Lord, the same spirit actuates the whole profession.'

Nelson arrived back at Portsmouth on 14 September. He had intended to walk to the sally port a few hundred yards away at the end of the High Street to be rowed out to his flagship, but a large crowd had gathered, making passage impossible. He slipped out of a back door and headed towards the beach at Southsea but according to an American visitor, 'By the time he had arrived on the beach some hundreds of people had collected in his train, pressing all around and pushing to get a little before him to obtain a sight of his face. ... As the barge in which he embarked pushed away from the shore, the people gave three cheers, which his lordship returned by waving his hat.' Nelson turned to Hardy and remarked, 'I had their huzzas before – I have their hearts now.'

Nelson was rowed out to the ship anchored off the Isle of Wight, and he arrived on board at 11.30, when the flag of a vice-admiral was hoisted at the head of *Victory's* foremast. At eight in the morning of Sunday the 15th, the *Victory's* anchor was raised and she sailed out of the Solent in company with Blackwood's frigate, the *Euryalus*. He sent the *Euryalus* on ahead to Collingwood, ordering him that no gun salutes were to take place when he joined, and there was to be no hoisting of colors – 'it is well not to proclaim to the Enemy every ship which may join the Fleet'. On 28 September, he found the fleet off the Spanish coast and took command of a force of twenty-nine ships of the line. He wrote to his friend Sir John Acton, 'after being only twenty-five days in England, I find myself again in command of the Mediterranean Fleet. I only hope that I may be able, in a small degree, to fulfill the expectations of my country.'

In the fleet he found some old friends, such as Cuthbert Collingwood, who was to be his second-in-command. He found some divisions, for Sir Robert Calder was to go home to face a court martial on his conduct of the action against Villeneuve, and there was debate about which ships and captains should go with him. He found new friends, for example Captain George Duff of HMS *Mars* who wrote to his wife that Nelson was 'certainly the pleasantest Admiral I ever served under'.

Nelson rejected St Vincent's idea of close blockade, for again he hoped to lure the enemy out. The main fleet was stationed about forty miles from Cadiz, with a line of frigates and ships of the line, including Blackwood's *Euryalus* and

'As the barge in which he embarked pushed away from the shore, the people gave three cheers, which his lordship returned by waving his hat.' Nelson turned to Hardy and remarked, 'I had their huzzas before – I have their hearts now.'

Duff's *Mars*, stationed between them and the port to pass on signals if the enemy made any move. Thus the Combined Fleet would never be fully aware of his strength.

Nelson was an instinctive rather than a theoretical tactician. He had discussed his ideas with Captain Richard Keats at Merton during the peace, but nothing was written down. Immediately after joining his new fleet, he explained his tactics to his captains. 'The Nelson touch' was 'like an electric shock. Some shed tears, all approved – It was new – it was singular – it was simple!' A few days later he put his thoughts on paper and distributed them to his captains. He expected to have a fleet of forty sail, which would be impossible to form a single line of battle in time to beat the enemy. He would divide it into three squadrons, two of sixteen ships each. These would cut through the enemy line, isolating a portion of his rear, while the Advanced Squadron of 'eight of the fastest sailing Two-decked ships' would be ready to operate where most needed. It implied a headlong attack on the enemy, considerable initiative to the second-in-command of the fleet and the leader of the Advanced Squadron. But when battle actually threatened, Nelson had only twenty-seven ships of the line. He decided to attack in two lines.

At 9.30 on the morning of 19 October, HMS *Mars* repeated Blackwood's signal to the *Victory* that the enemy fleet was coming out of harbour. Villeneuve had been goaded by Napoleon into risking battle though he had no confidence in his own men. He knew that Nelson had sent one of his squadrons to Gibraltar to water, and believed that his strength was much reduced, so Nelson's blockading tactics were successful. The movements of the Combined Fleet were slow and Nelson had plenty of time to prepare himself, his men and ships for battle and possible death. Once out of Cadiz the Combined Fleet headed south-east to attempt to enter the Mediterranean, still unaware of Nelson's strength.

Nelson rose soon after dawn on the 21st and came on deck 'dressed as usual in his Admiral's frock-coat, bearing on the left breast four stars of the different orders which he always wore with his common apparel'. He was in good spirits and told Hardy that he would not be satisfied with capturing less than twenty sail of the line. At 6.40 he ordered the hoisting of the signal 'prepare for battle'.

At this point Nelson signalled Captain Blackwood to come on board the flagship, along with the three other frigate captains, to 'talk and explain to me what he expected from the frigates in and after the action; to thank me, which he did but too lavishly, for the service I had afforded him, the intelligence and look-out we had kept; and to tell me, if he lived, he should send me home with dispatches' – a great honour, which would have led to a knighthood for the messenger. Nelson kept Blackwood on board until the last minute, in case any further instructions were needed.

Blackwood and Hardy were concerned about the position of the *Victory* at the head of one of the lines, where she would attract most of the enemy's fire during the approach. They suggested that he might transfer his flag to the *Euryalus* where he would be in less danger. Nelson would not hear of it, so they tried to persuade him to let one of the other large ships take the lead. Nelson agreed and Blackwood was sent over to the *Temeraire* with the message, but meanwhile an officer found that one of the *Victory's* studding sails was badly set and took it in to reset it. Nelson thought he was reducing sail without orders. The sail was replaced and the *Victory* drew ahead of the *Temeraire*. Blackwood returned to find that Nelson was setting more sail and the *Temeraire* could not overtake.

The Admiral began to make his personal preparations. Recognising the possibility of death he wrote a codicil to his will, witnessed by Hardy and Blackwood. Emma Hamilton's 'services to the nation' at Naples and elsewhere

Victory Oct.[r] 19: 1805
Noon Cadiz ESE 16 Leagues

My Dearest beloved Emma the dear friend of my bosom the signal has been made that the Enemys combined fleet are coming out of Port, we have very little Wind so that I have no hopes of seeing them before tomorrow may the God of Battles crown my endeavours with success at all events I will take care that my name shall ever be most dear to you and Horatia both of whom I love as much as my own life, and as my last writing before the battle will be to you so I hope in God that I shall live to finish my letter after the

Nelson's last letter to Lady Hamilton, written as he received news that the enemy fleet was coming out.
The British Library, Egerton MS 1614, f.125

were recommended for attention, and he left her 'a Legacy to my King and Country, that they will give her an ample provision to maintain her rank in life'. Horatia Nelson Thompson his 'adopted' daughter was to use the name of Nelson only. He wrote in his private diary:

> May the Great God, whom I worship, grant to my Country, and for the benefit of Europe in general, a great and glorious Victory; and may no misconduct in any one tarnish it; and may humanity after Victory be the predominant feature in the British Fleet. For myself, individually, I commit my life to Him who made me, and may his blessing light upon my endeavours for serving my Country faithfully. To Him I resign myself and the just cause which is entrusted to me to defend. Amen, Amen, Amen.

Lieutenant Pasco, the signal officer, was concerned with his own position in the ship and resolved to speak to Nelson about it. 'On entering the cabin, I discovered his Lordship on his knees writing [for the furniture had been cleared away for battle]. He was then penning that beautiful Prayer. I waited until he rose and communicated what I had to report, but could not at such a moment, disturb his mind with any grievances of mine.'

Nelson's uniform, though not the full dress of an admiral, might attract the attention of enemy marksmen by its epaulettes and stars. Some of his officers wanted him to cover them, but when Surgeon Beatty suggested this, John Scott the Secretary replied 'Take care, Doctor, what you are about: I would not be the man to mention such a matter to him'.

Around 11.30 the admiral ordered the signal officer to send a 'fillip' to his men. 'Mr. Pasco, I wish to say to the fleet, "England confides [i.e. is confident that] that every man will do his duty."' Pasco pointed out that in the new signal code all the words could be made by three-number hoists, except 'confides' and 'duty', which would have to be spelled letter by letter. He suggested 'expects' instead of 'confides' and Nelson agreed. In the *Royal Sovereign*, Collingwood's first reaction to the flurry of flags was to say 'that he wished Nelson would make no more signals, for they all understood what they were to do'. He changed his mind when he saw the message and 'expressed great delight and admiration'. Lieutenant Cumby of the *Bellerophon* agreed that it 'produced the most animating and inspiriting effect on the whole fleet'.

The enemy had now turned back and was trying to get back to Cadiz. The thirty-three ships of the line were in a loose crescent formation, with French and Spanish intermingled, and several gaps and overlaps. As the British ships approached at speeds of three or four knots, Nelson had to decide exactly where his line should attack. One possibility was to cut it at about a third of the way from the head, sealing off a section to be eliminated by him and Collingwood. Another was to head for the enemy flagship, probably in the centre of the line. But the allied fleet had still not hoisted its flags. Was Villeneuve still in command, in his old flagship, the *Bucentaure*? Or had another admiral taken over, perhaps with his flag in the largest ship in the fleet, the unmistakable *Santisima Trinidad*? Clearly the enemy was retreating towards Cadiz, but would he continue to do so when that seemed increasingly unlikely to succeed? Nelson feared that a large part of the fleet would escape, so for a time he sailed to intercept the head of the Franco–Spanish line, abandoning the idea of containment. Far from being pre-arranged, his plan of attack evolved continually during the approach.

At around midday Collingwood's *Royal Sovereign*, at the head of the other line, was the first British ship to engage in what became the Battle of Trafalgar. As she came close to the enemy line, several ships opened fire. At that moment the British ships broke out their white ensigns on their sterns, supplemented by union flags hung from the rigging. Nelson was determined to prevent confusion in the fog of war. The *Victory* entered the action about ten minutes after the *Royal Sovereign*, as the shots of several enemy ships began to reach her, making the most impression on her fore topsail. Fifteen minutes later she opened fire and attempted to pass through the enemy line, which closed up to resist her. She found herself closely engaged with the French ships *Bucentaure* and *Redoutable*. The latter ship was particularly dangerous in the circumstances, for her captain had decided to neglect his heavy guns in favour of musketry from the decks and tops, to be followed by boarding. A shot struck the deck between Hardy and the admiral, who remarked, 'This is too warm work, Hardy, to last long'. At about 1.15, after about an hour of close action, a musket ball from *Redoutable*'s mizzen top hit Nelson on the left shoulder, passed through his lung and broke his backbone.

Nelson was quickly lifted up by Sergeant Secker of the Royal Marines and two seamen, and carried excruciatingly down four steep ladderways to the cockpit in the bowels of the ship. Probably it was instinctive reaction, for wounded men were always carried below. Yet it had two unfortunate effects. It could only have worsened the spinal injury, and it denied Nelson the chance to die among his men, on the battlefield that was *Victory's* quarterdeck. Nelson was constantly spurting blood, in great agony, and his lungs were filling up with his own blood. The famous words on his deathbed were issued in gasps, not articulated serenely as the written record seems to suggest.

Nelson was tended by Beatty the surgeon and Scott the chaplain, and lay against a knee on the side of the ship, among the other wounded. Hardy had to attend to duties on deck, especially since the fleet would look to *Victory* for signals until Collingwood could take over. He visited Nelson after an hour or so and told the admiral that twelve or fourteen ships had surrendered. Nelson had hoped for twenty. On his next visit Nelson's condition was far worse and he was in obvious pain and distress. He ordered Hardy to anchor after the battle, since a storm was approaching. He was concerned that he might be thrown overboard, as

At about 1.15, after about an hour of close action, a musket ball from *Redoutable*'s mizzen top hit Nelson on the left shoulder, passed through his lung and broke his backbone.

the dead often were in battle; but there was no question of that. He urged Hardy to take care of Lady Hamilton, and asked him to kiss him. After that, he said 'Thank God I have done my duty.' Hardy went back on deck filled with emotion, and within fifteen minutes Nelson was unable to speak. He died at about half-past four, after two-and-three-quarter hours of agony.

The death of Nelson had no material effect on the action, and no moral effect while it was still unknown to the majority of officers and crews. In the mêlée battle there was little more for an admiral to do once the fight had been joined, especially in light winds and poor visibility caused by gunsmoke. The first British ships in action were isolated and suffered heavy casualties, but gave as good as they got until the other ships arrived to gain complete superiority over the enemy in five hours of battle. In all twenty ships of the Combined Fleet were taken, though all but four of the prizes were lost in storms which followed the battle.

Some French writers have implied that Nelson's death cancelled out the victory. If so, then his life must have been extraordinarily valuable. More accurately, we can see the battle for what it was, a crushing victory for the British, marred by the strategic cost and personal tragedy of the death of a great warrior and a beloved hero. Even this strategic loss was not as serious as it might have been, for Nelson's work was essentially done. There were no more enemy fleets to defeat. No-one dared to risk a fleet battle with the British for the rest of the war, which lasted a further nine years. Enemy strategy was severely hampered.

Nelson's attitudes had a great effect on the navy of the day. In July 1805 Sir John Calder believed that he had done quite well in stopping Villeneuve's fleet off Finisterre, and he wrote expectantly to the Admiralty hinting at rewards. But there was a whispering campaign against him in the fleet, and he insisted on a court martial to clear his name. In the meantime Trafalgar was fought and again

Devis's famous painting of the death of
Nelson greatly exaggerates the height
between the decks in the cockpit of the
Victory. Captain Hardy is the tall figure
to the right of Nelson.
*National Maritime Museum, Greenwich
Hospital Collection BHC 2894*

Nelson showed what a naval victory really meant. Poor Calder was reprimanded
for his failure to produce a great victory, and Nelson's credo of 1795 – 'had we
taken ten sail, and allowed the 11th to escape when it had been possible to have
got at her, I could never have called it well done' – was now the standard by
which naval achievement would be measured.

Nelson's funeral, in twentieth-century terms, might be seen as a
combination of those of Sir Winston Churchill and Princess Diana – the warrior
who had saved his country and the beloved but flawed popular icon. The body
was brought home in a cask of brandy, and it lay in state in the Naval Hospital,

An invitation to Nelson's funeral on 10 January 1806. Thousands of people joined the procession through London to pay their respects.
The British Library, Additional MS 46358, f.170

Greenwich. It was borne into a barge for a procession up the Thames to London. On 10 January 1806 a great procession left the Admiralty Building in Whitehall, so long that its head had completed the journey before the tail had left. By his own request Nelson was buried in St Paul's Cathedral, for he believed that Westminster Abbey was built on marshy ground and would not survive.

An admiral does not leave such a permanent legacy as a writer or a painter. Statesmen leave laws and policies. Even a soldier might conquer territory which becomes a permanent part of the nation, but a sailor fights on an uninhabited and fluid medium. The ripples of a great naval victory are likely to die down over the years, and its meaning is diluted by subsequent events. This is less true of Nelson than any other admiral.

Nelson's legacy to the British nation, apart from the immediate results of his great battles, is complex. He gave the Royal Navy an ideal of complete and uncompromising victory which has survived the centuries. His personal reputation has risen and fallen over the years and his private life made him unacceptable for much of the Victorian era. The Royal Navy idolised him in the First World War, but created an inflexible tactical system which he would have deplored, and failed to win victory at Jutland in 1916. In the second great war of the twentieth century it was probably the junior officers – submarine and destroyer captains and Fleet Air Arm pilots – who showed the Nelson spirit most effectively.

For the British nation as a whole, Nelson's column stands in the centre of London, though not everyone thinks about its significance. Apart from Drake and Cook, his is the only name which is remembered from the Royal Navy in the age of sail. Nelson's personality still attracts people of many different backgrounds, and to them Trafalgar Day, with the death of its hero and its ambiguous victory, is a day of commemoration.

Chronology

1795	13–14 March: Hotham's Action in which Nelson captured two French ships
	13 July: Hotham's Second Action, an indecisive battle
	11 August: Appointed commodore
	30 November: Sir John Jervis takes command of the Mediterranean Fleet
1796	11 June: Transferred to the 74-gun ship *Captain*
	20 October: Completes evacuation of Corsica
	19–20 December: Encounter with Spanish frigates
	27 December: Arrives at Elba to begin evacuation of the island
1797	14 February: Battle of St Vincent in which Nelson initiated the main attack and captured two Spanish ships
	20 February: Promoted to rear-admiral
	3–5 July: Unsuccessful attack on Spanish at Cadiz
	24 July: Lost right arm in attack on Tenerife
	19 December: Gives thanks for recovery from his wound
1798	30 April: Joined St Vincent's fleet off Cadiz in the *Vanguard* of 74 guns
	20 May: The *Vanguard* severely damaged in a storm off Toulon
	7 June: Joined by a force under Captain Troubridge
	28 June: Failed to find the French at Alexandria
	2 August: Battle of the Nile. Nelson is wounded in the head but captures or destroys twelve enemy ships of the line
	22 September: Arrived at Naples to stay with Sir William and Lady Hamilton
	28 November: Captured Livorno (Leghorn)
	23 December: Sailed for Palermo with the Neapolitan Royal Family
1799	25 June: Arrived off Naples to support the Royalists. Refused to accept the terms of surrender of the Republican rebels
1800	30 March: In the *Foudroyant*, in company with other ships, captured the French *Guillaume Tell* which had escaped from the Battle of the Nile
	17 July: Began his journey home overland with the Hamiltons
	6 November: Landed at Great Yarmouth
1801	1 January: Promoted to vice-admiral
	13 January: Separated from Lady Nelson
	Late January: Horatia, daughter of Nelson and Lady Hamilton, born in London

12 March: In the *St George* of 98 guns, sailed with Sir Hyde Parker for the Baltic

2 April: Battle of Copenhagen

24 July: Appointed commander-in-chief of a squadron to prevent French invasion

16 August: Unsuccessful attack on the French at Boulogne

22 October: Began leave of absence

1802 July and August: Tour of Wales with Sir William and Lady Hamilton

1803 6 April: Death of Sir William Hamilton

16 May: Appointed commander-in-chief, Mediterranean Fleet, in the 100-gun *Victory*

8 July: Arrived on station off Toulon in the frigate *Amphion*

1804 With Mediterranean Fleet in the *Victory*, patrolling off Toulon and at anchorages in Sardinia

1805 19 January: Off Sardinia, received information that the French fleet was out

8 February: Off Alexandria seeking the French, who had actually returned to Toulon

4 April: Off Sardinia, received news that the French Fleet was out

11 May: Began voyage to the West Indies in pursuit of the French

4 June: Arrived at Barbados

7 June: Anchored at Trinidad in the mistaken belief that the French were attacking the island

13 June: Sailed from Antigua

19 July: Off Gibraltar

19 August: Went to live at Merton with Lady Hamilton

14 September: Rejoined the *Victory* at Portsmouth

28 September: Joined the fleet off Cadiz

21 October: Battle of Trafalgar and the death of Nelson

23 December: Nelson's body arrives at Greenwich

1806 9 January: Buried in St Paul's Cathedral, London

Glossary

Bold type denotes an entry for the subject elsewhere in the glossary.

Admiral
A senior officer in the navy, eligible to command a fleet or a squadron rather than a single ship. In Nelson's time there were nine grades, and promotion from one grade to another was by seniority. Starting with the lowest, the grades were:
Rear-admiral of the blue
Rear-admiral of the white
Rear-admiral of the red
Vice-admiral of the blue
Vice-admiral of the white
Vice-admiral of the red
Admiral of the blue
Admiral of the white
Admiral of the fleet.

Aft
Towards the rearmost part or stern of a ship.

Bow
The foremost part of a ship, the part which is the first to penetrate the water when under way.

Bowsprit
A spar which projects diagonally ahead of the bow of a sailing ship. It is able to carry some sails, either above or below it.

Brig
A vessel, usually small with two masts, both square rigged; that is, with the mast hung from yards set across the ship rather than running fore and aft as in a cutter or a schooner.

Broadside
The guns on one side of a warship, or a volley of shot from them.

Captain
A senior officer, eligible to command a **rated** ship, also known as a post captain. Colloquially, any officer in command of a warship, whether he holds the rank of captain or not. Also, the man in charge of a merchant ship.

Commander
Originally 'master and commander'. A rank between lieutenant and captain, held by an officer who could command a ship that was too small to be **rated**.

Commodore
A temporary rank between captain and rear-admiral. The holder was entitled to fly a flag known as a 'broad pennant' from the mast of his ship.

Coxswain
A seaman in charge of a small boat. A captain or admiral had his own coxswain who would have him rowed ashore or to other ships.

Flag captain
The captain of a **flagship**, often the confidant of the admiral on board.

Flagship
A warship, usually one of the largest ones in the fleet, which carries an admiral and his staff. So called because the admiral flies his distinguishing flag from one of the masts.

Forward
Towards the bows or forward part of a ship.

Frigate
A medium-sized warship, smaller than a **ship of the line**, with a single deck of guns and good sailing qualities. Used for many purposes such as reconnaissance, convoy escort, commerce raiding, patrols and carrying messages.

Gunboat
A very small warship, often armed with a single gun pointing forward.

Jolly-boat
A small boat, about 18 feet (5.5 metres) long, carried by a larger ship.

Larboard
Obsolete term for port, or left.

Lieutenant
The most junior rank of commissioned officer. The first lieutenant is the second-in-command and administrative officer of a ship, the others take turns as officer of the watch.

Lower deck
The ordinary sailors, marines, artisans, servants, etc of a ship, who normally lived on the lower deck of a two- or three-decked ship.

Merchant navy
The commercial shipping of a country, made up of a large number of privately owned passenger and cargo ships (merchantmen) and fishing vessels.

Midshipman
A man, usually but not always young, who is training to become a commissioned officer.

Mizzen
The aftermost and smallest of the three masts on a typical ship of the period.

Poop
A short deck on a ship of the line or large merchant ship, the aftermost and highest deck.

Post-captain
See **Captain**.

Privateer
A privately-owned warship, which made a profit by capturing enemy ships and selling them and their cargoes.

Quarter galleries
Galleries projecting from each side of the stern of a ship, often used as toilet accommodation for the officers.

Quarterdeck
A deck running for about half of the length of a ship, on which the steering wheel is normally fitted and from which the ship is controlled. On a frigate it was the highest and furthest aft deck, on a ship of the line it was below the poop. Figuratively it refers to the officers of a ship, as distinct from the **lower deck**.

Rates
Ships with more than 20 guns were rated as follows:
First rate:
    100 plus guns and 850 plus men
Second rate:
    90–98 guns and 750 men
Third rate:
    64–84 guns and 500–720 men
Fourth rate:
    50–60 guns and 350–420 men
Fifth rate:
    30–44 guns and 215–294 men
Sixth rate:
    20–28 guns and 121–195 men
The rate served mainly to establish the pay and numbers of certain officers. Ships of the fourth rate and above were normally regarded as **ships of the line**. **Frigates** were usually fifth rates. Ships were also known by the number of guns they carried, e.g. a 74-gun ship; or by the number of complete decks of guns, e.g. the *Victory* was a three-decker.

Schooner
A small or medium-sized ship, usually American in Nelson's day, with at least two masts, all rigged with fore-and-aft sails and therefore able to sail close to the wind.

Seaman
Generally, anyone including officers who followed the profession of the sea. More specifically it meant the men of the **lower deck** who had served some time at sea. They were rated as able seamen if they had considerable experience and skill, as ordinary seamen if they had served about two years and demonstrated their competence, and as landsmen if they had no experience or skills.

Ship of the line
A ship big and powerful enough to stand in the line of battle with similar ships, where it might be expected to hold its place against the very largest of the enemy. Though fourth **rates** were still technically ships of the line in Nelson's time, the 64-gun ship was regarded as the smallest practicable ship. There was no upper limit to the size.

Stern
The rear part of a ship.

Strike one's flag
When an admiral leaves his ship or his post, the flag is lowered or 'struck' with some ceremony.

Underwater lines
The shape of a ship's hull underwater, which can have a crucial effect on her sailing qualities.

Wardroom
A room on the upper deck at the stern of a ship of the line, used as a dining and common room for the lieutenants and marine officers and specialist officers such as the master, surgeon and purser.

Further reading

The *Despatches and Letters of Vice Admiral Lord Viscount Nelson* was published in seven volumes by Sir Nicholas Harris Nicolas in 1844 and reprinted in the same format by Chatham Publishing in 1997–98. The title understates the scope of the work, which contains many documents not by Nelson himself, particularly in relation to his battles. In the eleventh edition of the *Encyclopaedia Britannica* of 1911 David Hannay wrote, 'The student of Nelson's life should make it a rule to exhaust Nicolas before consulting any other authority.' This is still largely true, despite the publication of several other volumes of letters. A proposed new collection, to be published in 2005 edited by Colin White, will reveal many new letters.

Original Nelson Material

The bulk of Nelson's letters are to be found in The British Library, with important collections in the Nelson Museum at Monmouth and the National Maritime Museum, Greenwich. The latter institution has just acquired collections of his prize papers after the Nile and letters from Lady Nelson, which may add much to our understanding of his life.

G.P.B. Naish, ed, *Nelson's Letters to his Wife and Other Documents, 1785–1831*, Navy Records Society, 1958. Again the title understates the size of the work, which also contains important correspondence on, for example, the Nile Campaign.

Modern Nelson Biographies

Tom Pocock, *Horatio Nelson*, Bodley Head, London, 1987

Terry Coleman, *The Nelson Touch, the Life and Legend of Horatio Nelson*, Oxford University Press, Oxford, 2002

David Howarth and Stephen Howarth, *Nelson, the Immortal Memory*, J.M. Dent, London, 1988

Individual Episodes in Nelson's Life

Tom Pocock, *The Young Nelson in the Americas*, Collins, London, 1980

Colin White, 1797, *Nelson's Year of Destiny*, Sutton, Stroud, 1998

Brian Lavery, *Nelson and the Nile*, Chatham Publishing, London, 1998

Flora Fraser, *Beloved Emma, the Life of Emma, Lady Hamilton*, Weidenfeld and Nicolson, London, 1998

Dudley Pope, *The Great Gamble*, Weidenfeld and Nicolson, London, 1972

Sir Julian Corbett, *The Campaign of Trafalgar*, Longmans, Green, London, 1910

David Howarth, *Trafalgar, the Nelson Touch*, Collins, Glasgow, 1969

Background Works

John Ehrman, *The Younger Pitt, Vol Two, The Reluctant Transition*, Constable, London, 1983 and *Vol Three, The Consuming Struggle*, Constable, London, 1996

William James, *The Naval History of Great Britain*, Vols I to III, Conway Maritime Press, reprinted London, 2002

Brian Lavery, *Nelson's Navy, the Ships, Men and Organisation*, Conway Maritime Press, London, 1989

Index

These are to certify that Vincenza Grau[...]
5 feet 7 inches high born [...]
came before me and declar[...]
enlisted himself to serve his [...]
in His Royal Marine Forces [...]
the second and third articles [...]
Desertion were likewise read [...]
oath of Fidelity mention'd [...]
have examined the [...]
said Vincenza Grauvenor Knabe
and [...] him in every
respect fit for His
[Majes]ty's Service -

[signature]